ACHIEVING SUCCESSFUL TRANSITIONS

for young people with disabilities

of related interest

Personalisation in Practice
Supporting Young People with Disabilities
through the Transition to Adulthood
Suzie Franklin with Helen Sanderson
Foreword by Nicola Gitsham
ISBN 978 1 84905 443 0
eISBN 978 0 85700 816 9

Active Support
Enabling and Empowering People
with Intellectual Disabilities
Jim Mansell and Julie Beadle-Brown
ISBN 978 1 84905 111 8
eISBN 978 0 85700 300 3

JILL HUGHES

NATALIE LACKENBY

ACHIEVING SUCCESSFUL TRANSITIONS

for young people with disabilities

A PRACTICAL GUIDE

Jessica Kingsley *Publishers*
London and Philadelphia

Contains public sector information licensed under the Open Government Licence v3.0.

First published in 2015
by Jessica Kingsley Publishers
73 Collier Street
London N1 9BE, UK
and
400 Market Street, Suite 400
Philadelphia, PA 19106, USA

www.jkp.com

Library of Congress Cataloging in Publication Data
Hughes, Jill, 1976-
 Achieving successful transitions for young people with disabilities
: a practical guide / Jill Hughes and Natalie Lackenby.
   pages cm
 Includes bibliographical references and index.
 ISBN 978-1-84905-568-0 (alk. paper)
 1. Youth with disabilities--Services for--Great Britain. 2. Youth with disabilities--Vocational education--Great Britain. 3. Youth with disabilities--Education--Great Britain. 4. School-to-work transition--Great Britain. I. Lackenby, Natalie. II. Title.
 HV1569.3.Y68H84 2015
 362.40835'0941--dc23
                    2014048028

British Library Cataloguing in Publication Data
A CIP catalogue record for this book is available from the British Library

ISBN 978 1 84905 568 0
eISBN 978 1 78450 005 4

Printed and bound in Great Britain

CONTENTS

ACKNOWLEDGEMENTS

We would like to thank the Young Adults Team in Worcestershire for all of your help, support and professional input. And for putting up with us moaning! Particular thanks to our team manager, Jonathan Monk, for his chapter contribution as well as his continued support, positivity and goodwill. Special thanks also to Alessandra Parsons and Emily Jesson for their support and for organising us!

1

WHY IS ACHIEVING SUCCESSFUL TRANSITIONS FOR YOUNG PEOPLE WITH DISABILITIES SO IMPORTANT?

JONATHAN MONK

INTRODUCTION

'Transition' is defined as the movement, passage or change from one position, state or stage to another. Transitions, both planned and unplanned, are an inevitable part of everyday life and cannot be avoided or prevented. Indeed, transitions are a time of celebration, where change can be positive and liberating. However, it should also be recognised that transitions can present significant challenges for some people. In the social care context, transition has a particular meaning, and is generally considered in relation to specific practice themes, such as the transition from adolescence to adulthood (Lauerman 2014).

For young people and their families, the transition from school to adulthood is crucial for achieving a good life and for securing a positive future. It is a time of celebration, change, choice, decision-making and challenge for all young people. Young people frequently talk about wanting to be able to move into adult life with real opportunities for getting a job; having access to a range of housing options; living healthy lives; and having relationships and a social life in the community. This applies equally to young people with disabilities, but they frequently describe the process as a particularly difficult, uncertain and stressful time. Indeed, young people and their families will often explain how worried they become as they prepare to leave school and move on from children's services to face what they describe as a 'cliff edge' of uncertainty about what support may be available in the future (Lee 2012).

The evidence shows that support available for young people and their families through the transition process varies greatly (DCSF and DH 2007), despite the increased prominence of transition in policy and legislation, and the growing evidence base to support the importance of person-centred transition planning (DH 2011).

Indeed, the business case for statutory services to ensure effective transition planning is all too clear: the population of children and young people with disabilities across the UK is estimated at over 7770,000, and the evidence suggests that this number is rising (DH 2007b). It is estimated that there are 286,000 children aged 0–17 in the UK with a learning disability (Foundation for People with Learning Disabilities 2011). Approximately 200,000 children in England are currently at the School Action Plus stage of assessment of special educational needs (SEN) or have a Statement of SEN (Foundation for People with Learning Disabilities 2011). In their study on estimating the future need for adult social care services for people with learning disabilities in England, Emerson and Hatton (2008, p.15) suggest 'sustained growth' in the need for social care over the time period up to 2026. The study projects annual increases from 3.20 per cent at the lower estimate to 7.94 per cent at the higher estimate. Young people making the transition from children's services, increasing rates of maternal employment, improvements in healthcare and support for young people with complex health needs and changing expectations among families are seen as some of the primary factors contributing to these increases (Emerson and Hatton 2008). The Department of Health (2007b) indicates that the increase is also due to other factors such as greater numbers of children and young people being identified as having autistic spectrum conditions.

As such, the estimates suggest that social care would be required to support between 47,000 to 113,000 additional adults with learning disabilities over the next 10 years (DH 2007b). All of this indicates a growing pressure on statutory services to examine their arrangements for transition planning, as this is likely to be a key pressure point for capacity and funding.

Given these considerations, if achieving successful transitions is so crucial for young people, their families and the agencies that support them, the question remains, why is it so difficult to get it right?

This chapter focuses on what is involved in order to achieve successful transition planning for young people, their families and for the services and agencies responsible for supporting them. It examines the process of transition and the impact of a changing policy framework that focuses on more effective transition planning and improving outcomes for young people. It goes on to consider whether this increased profile has truly promoted the voices of young people in their transition plan. A detailed analysis of the strategies and initiatives that have been implemented to improve the experience of young people and their families within the transition process follows. The chapter then outlines how agencies can better commission services and ensure value for money and cost-effectiveness on a macro level as a result of effective transition planning.

WHY IS TRANSITION SO DIFFICULT TO GET RIGHT?

Transition occurs at different stages in the young person's life, including when they leave school, turn 18 and/or leave college or home for the first time. The process is generally started when the young person is at school, usually in Year 9 (around age 14), when they should have a *transition review* held by the school. Most importantly, the transition review must involve young people and their families in the process, by giving them an opportunity to share their needs, views, hopes, fears and aspirations for the future (Kaehne and Beyer 2011). The review is also the point at which the different strands of assessment and planning need to come together. As such, the all-encompassing nature of the transitions process requires coordination from a range of professionals and agencies with clear pathways through health, social care, housing, education and community services in order to ensure that young people can achieve their full potential as they move into adulthood (explored more fully in Chapter 2).

Yet in reality, experience and evidence finds that young people with disabilities face 'multiple barriers' that make it more difficult to achieve their potential to achieve the outcomes they should be seeking (Broadhurst, Yates and Mullen 2012, p.125) – not least, the disjointed and variable range of support available to them across community and statutory services (Audit Commission 2007).

This can result in significant costs for young people, families and statutory services alike, including the following:

- There are missed opportunities and lost potential for young people to achieve independent living and to engage in education, employment and training.

- Transition becomes a process that happens to young people rather than one that involves and engages them in planning, and that offers real choice and control.

- Young people and families become disaffected and dissatisfied.

- Decision-making can have long-term, and in some cases, lifelong, implications for the young person.

- Commissioning with limited time and in emergencies is likely to result in inappropriate, costly and restrictive services, making it difficult to secure value for money and good use of resources.

- There is reduced ability for creative transition support planning that maximises the use of everyday community services and natural/ informal support from within the family or community networks.

- Ultimately, young people 'fall through the net'.

Indeed, Morris (1999, cited in Broadhurst *et al.* 2012) highlights that one of the outcomes of poor transition planning is very few young people with a disability having a paid job. Instead, many find themselves accessing traditional day centres with paid employment not routinely considered as part of transition. Morris goes on to highlight that for many young people, a specialist college is often the expected route of progression from school, regardless of whether that is the young person's choice or aspiration, and there is little emphasis on leisure, friendships and personal relationships. In reality, many specialist colleges are geographically distant from the young people's home locations, and include a residential element. So their social networks and any friendships gained while at school frequently disappear and are difficult to re-establish following the end of their course, should they return back to their home locality. Beresford and Cavet (2009) highlight that in these circumstances, some young people will be affected by feelings of loneliness and isolation, the loss of friends and changes to relationships, and anxiety about changes to and loss of routine, structure, familiarity and predictability on which many aspects of their lives may have previously been based.

The transition from specialist college can also be problematic in relation to longer-term housing options, where the decision about where to live is often determined by what vacancies are available in more traditional group home settings than by young people's choice about where to live and with whom. It can therefore be seen that transition involves emotional costs for some young people as a result of change in new living situations, routines and circumstances (explored more fully in Chapter 6).

In this context, the specific needs of young people with disabilities in the looked-after system should also be considered. The National Care Advisory Service (2009) indicates that this is a diverse group of young people with different needs for support and with differing levels of practical and emotional development to live independently. As such, each young person has specific needs relating to transition planning. Cocker and Allain (2008) suggest that some of the challenges for this group of young people relate to feeling constrained and limited in what is available to them; conflict with families and professionals about the levels of care, support and in some cases surveillance that they need; and a desire to have greater levels of independence and intimate adult relationships. As part of successful transition planning, it is crucial to find ways to meaningfully engage with these young people to find out from them what their wishes and feelings are so that their views form the basis for decision-making, while also ensuring that appropriate safeguards can be put in place. This is a delicate balance that takes time, risk assessment and negotiation to do effectively (discussed further in Chapter 3).

The Children (Leaving Care) Act 2000 introduced significant new duties requiring local authorities to continue to support young people who are looked-after into adulthood. They are entitled to a needs assessment leading to a pathway plan, and also have the right to access support from a personal adviser. Local authorities must also provide assistance (and financial support) in relation to education, training or employment, as provided for in the young person's pathway plan.

Transition is not a stand-alone process or a one-off episode, and the Year 9 transition review should be seen merely as the starting point and not the main event. It should be a fluid process that is spread over a number of years. Young people are likely to experience multiple transitions occurring independently of each other, which will involve them having to engage with new agencies and professionals, and therefore having to re-tell their story each time, which can, of course, bring with it stress, anxiety and frustration. This is compounded by poor communication across professions and agencies. In the transition toolkit *Pathways to Getting a Life*, Getting a Life (GAL), Helen Sanderson Associates (HSA) and the National Development Team for inclusion (NDTi) (2011, p.8) indicate that statutory agencies are 'weak' at communicating about transition planning, and operate very different cultures, systems, processes and working practices. Agencies operate different systems that don't share information or plans, and there is often a lack of shared understanding of priorities or agreement for risk-taking or resource allocation. This results in disjointed planning and unresponsive decision-making for young people and their families. This can also clearly result in a 'lack of engagement by some agencies with the process and will therefore affect the usefulness of the process for young people and the family in the long run' (Kaehne and Beyer 2011, p.29). GAL *et al.* (2011, p.9) set out that transition falls in the gap between children's and adult services, meaning that 'no one takes responsibility for making sure actions happen'.

As set out previously, the transition pathway is generally begun at school, and therefore schools and education play a critical role in achieving successful transition planning. However, schools may not always be as committed to person-centred transition planning as they should be. They may not invest sufficient time or support for young people to be effectively involved in setting out their views, needs and aspirations to be included in their transition plan, or transition review meetings may be inaccessible or stressful for the young person. Clearly, a 'one size fits all' approach to transition planning does not work. Young people and those working with them frequently have low expectations about what is possible, and there is often insufficient flexibility to help prepare young people for transition planning and to support them to define the outcomes they want to achieve (DH Partnerships for Children, Families and Maternity 2008). As a consequence, young people's transition plans can be professional-led and take the form of a 'shopping list' from a menu of existing inflexible and often outdated services rather than an opportunity to find out about what the young person wants to achieve in the future and how their strengths, skills, ideas and interests can be built on.

The role of parents and carers in achieving successful transitions is critical. However, for many parents, the transition process is a particularly difficult and stressful time (Parker 2014). Parents will frequently raise concerns about the young person's future and the transition process, including:

- the young person's ability to manage some or all aspects of their life

- concerns about funding issues for services or placements

- lack of progression from school and the absence of meaningful daytime occupation

- real or perceived increased vulnerability associated with independence and adulthood

- risk to mental health and wellbeing

- financial considerations and the fear of losing carers' benefits for themselves and/or disability benefits for the young person

- the parent's own ability to continue the caring role

- risk of the young person entering the criminal justice system.

Carpenter (1997, cited in Robinson 2000, p.24) suggests that transition planning should be *whole family focused* in which parents (and siblings, where appropriate) are viewed as making an 'invaluable contribution', with emphasis on collaboration with parents to work towards a *shared agenda and goals,* with an open and frank exchange of information. Carpenter goes on to stress the importance of 'effective ongoing evaluation' so that the transition plan can be reviewed and adjusted as needed in line with the young person's and family's changing circumstances and best interests. However, all of this requires a person-centred approach to transition, and the flexibility, adaptability and resources from professionals and agencies already identified as lacking in many situations.

However, concerns have also been raised about the risk of parents' and carers' views dominating transition planning, and where their needs are prioritised over those of the young person, particularly where the young person has specific communication needs. In such situations, it is argued that there is a significant risk of parents' own needs driving the decision-making process (Beresford *et al.* 2013). (Carers' issues and themes are explored more thoroughly in Chapter 9.)

This also needs to be considered in the context of the changing legal status of the young person as they move into adulthood, and the shift from the rights, duties, powers, responsibilities and authority by law that is covered by *parental responsibility,* as set out in the Children Act 1989. Under the provision of the Mental Capacity Act 2005, young people post-16 should be supported to make decisions for themselves, or to consider best interests decisions where this is not possible (see Chapter 8 for more information regarding mental capacity, and the issues that can present during transition). This is a challenging paradigm shift for many parents and carers who have previously been the *decision-makers,* and where the young person may have largely been dependent on that parent for many aspects of their life. Samuel (2012) sets out the provision under the Mental Capacity Act that parents should be advised of their rights to be consulted, and that they should start planning for decision-making as part of transition, so that they can 'empower their children to make decisions for themselves and make best interests decisions where this is not possible'. Parents and carers should be advised of their legal right to a separate assessment of their needs as *carers* as a distinct part of the transition process.

Young people and their families report a lack of timely and accessible information about planning, services and options (GAL *et al.* 2011). Indeed, professionals working across agencies also indicate that information is not readily available to them to support the young people and families with whom they work. This has a negative impact on their knowledge, confidence and skills to successfully support young people to navigate the often complex systems and processes that are involved. This lack of information is a key barrier that hampers confident, effective and creative person-centred transition planning. The lack of meaningful information about options such as direct payments and personal budgets is well documented (Davey *et al.* 2007), and prevents young people's transition plans from being truly outcome-focused, creative and personalised.

Despite the prominence of transition in recent legislation and policy, and the investment in programmes such as the National Transition Support Team and the Preparing for Adulthood programme, it can be argued that there is a lack of a coherent and strategic performance or quality framework to monitor the quality of person-centred transition planning. As a consequence, the variable nature of the way transitions are planned and developed with young people and their families by different agencies and across localities is compounded. The next section of this chapter sets out the context in which transitions support is delivered in order to highlight some key principles for best practice to achieve successful transition planning.

CHANGING LEGISLATIVE AND POLICY CONTEXT

The SEN Code of Practice (DfES 2001), under the provision of the Special Educational Needs and Disability Act 2001, placed new and increased emphasis on a transition plan that draws together information from a range of sources to plan coherently for the young person's move into adulthood. It sets out a range of principles that should 'underpin the nature' of transitions and transition plans, such as:

- Participative

- Holistic

- Supportive

- Evolving

- Inclusive

- Collaborative.

(DfES 2001, p.5)

The emphasis on the involvement of the young person and on collaboration with families and across professional boundaries and agencies is evident throughout the evolution of policy that governs transition. However, in practice, the effectiveness of the delivery of these principles remains patchy.

In 2001, the government White Paper, *Valuing People – A New Strategy for Learning Disability for the 21st Century*, set out a programme of action to enhance the lives of people with learning disabilities, with improving transition as one of the main priorities:

> As young people with disabilities move into adulthood to ensure continuity of care and support for the young person and their family and to provide equality of opportunities to enable as many young people as possible to participate in education, training and employment. (DH 2001, p.26)

The White Paper went on to recommend that person-centred planning should be in place for all young people moving to adult services, based on a set of key principles:

- The young person is at the centre – that is, they are consulted throughout the planning process and choose who else is involved.

- Family and friends are partners in planning.

- The plan reflects what is important to the young person (now or for the future).

- The plan reflects a capacity-based assessment on what the young person can do, alongside any support required.

- The plan helps build the young person's networks in the community and isn't focused on a range of available services.

- The plan requires ongoing listening, learning and action to put into action the support the young person needs to achieve what they want out of life.

However, Heslop et al. (2007, cited in Beresford and Cavet 2009) indicated that in reality there was very little evidence of person-centred approaches being reflected in transition planning. Indeed, in the same research, they suggest that the views of young people themselves and the people who knew them well were not always recognised or given proper attention. There is clear evidence that access to independent advocacy can promote the involvement of young people in transition planning, and can have a positive impact on the knowledge and behaviour of professionals to ensure a person-centred approach to transition. It can also be argued that involving advocates can highlight the need for an improved range of options for young people, and can support the confidence, self-esteem and personal development of the young person. However, despite these benefits, Townsley and Marriott (2010) found little evidence of young people having good access to independent advocacy at transition.

Since the launch in 2003 of *Every Child Matters* (HM Government 2003), the government programme for improving outcomes for all children, there has been a raft of policy initiatives and commitment introduced with the aim to improve the lives of children with disabilities and their families. However, the National Children's Bureau (NCB 2010, p.3) suggests that the intentions of such policies and initiatives have not been 'consistently translated into practice on the ground'.

The *National Service Framework for Children, Young People and Maternity Services* (in England), published in 2004 (DH 2004, Section 7), required local authorities and NHS trusts to ensure that 'transition planning has as its main focus the fulfilment of the hopes, dreams and potential of the disabled young person, in particular to maximise education, training and employment opportunities, to enjoy social relationships and to live independently'.

In 2005, the Prime Minister's Strategy Unit published *Improving the Life Chances of Disabled People*, a vision to ensure people with disabilities in the UK had access to the full opportunities and choices to improve their quality of life and be recognised as equal members of society. The vision identified transition as one of the priorities, and included planning for transition that is focused on individual needs, continuous service provision and access to a more transparent and appropriate menu of opportunities and choices as key ingredients for success.

The Aiming High for Disabled Children (AHDC) programme (NCB 2010) committed £340 million revenue funding from 2008 to 2011 to transform services for children with disabilities, with improving transition arrangements once again highlighted as a priority. The AHDC review found that more needed to be done to coordinate services for young people with disabilities in transition, and to ensure that the young people and their families had access to high-quality information at key points. To address this, the AHDC programme announced £19 million to develop a transition support programme with four main aims, to:

- support young people with disabilities to live the lives they want

- provide better support for young people with disabilities and their families

- change culture to improve local service delivery

- support every local area to share learning and improve.

While there was a positive response to the programme for going beyond the rhetoric as in other policies, and for providing financial support to a range of initiatives, concerns were raised about the short-term nature of the funding and the sustainability of the improvements once the AHDC monies had finished (Beresford *et al.* 2013).

The cross-government *Getting a Life* programme in 2011 highlighted that in the main, transition planning continued to fail to reflect the person-centred approaches that previous policy had anticipated. The programme focused on outcomes rather than services, but once again, ensuring local delivery of such an outcome-focused approach continued to be variable.

In March 2011, the government published the Green Paper, *Support and Aspiration: A New Approach to Special Educational Needs and Disability* (DfE 2011). It outlined proposals to reform the system of support for young people with SEN and disabilities and their families. A key strand was a single assessment process and the introduction of an Education, Health and Care (EHC) plan to bring together support for children and young people from birth to 25, focusing on outcomes beyond school or college. To support the delivery of these reforms, the Department for Education commissioned a number of projects, including the Preparing for Adulthood programme, to build on learning from previous initiatives and to share knowledge of best practice. The Preparing for Adulthood programme continues to provide resources and opportunities for networking and learning in order to support the implementation of the reforms, which, from September 2014, became statute under Part 3 of the Children and Families Act 2014.

The implementation of the Act, alongside Part 1 of the Care Act 2014 (to be implemented from April 2015), will fundamentally change the way transition is planned and the way support is provided. While the Children and Families Act introduces a system of support which extends from birth to 25 using an integrated Education, Health and Care (EHC) plan, the Care

Act relates to adult social care for people with care and support needs over the age of 18. There will therefore be a group of young people for whom both statutes will apply and interact. As such, the two Acts place similar emphasis on outcomes, personalisation and the integration of services. The provision for Education, Health ad Care (EHC) plans within the Children and Families Act sets out a single, coordinated assessment process, and strengthens the requirement for integration, collaboration and holistic assessment that has never truly been achieved by previous policy and legislation for transition. (These issues are explored in more depth in the next chapter.)

Personalisation and the use of direct payments and personal budgets as the mechanisms for providing personalised care and support are the cornerstones of both pieces of legislation. Young people and their families will have a right to request a personal budget as part of their EHC plan, and they will be able to use this in more creative ways to achieve a wider range of outcomes including education and health needs in addition to social care. (Chapter 4 examines personalisation more thoroughly in relation to transition.)

Continuity of care is also a key element of both Acts, whereby there is a clear requirement that no young person should find themselves without care or support as they make the transition to adult services. It is clear that there must be no gap in provision until a 'transition assessment' has been completed. As such, the Care Act requires local authorities to identify young people who have not previously received services, but where there is likely to be a *significant benefit* to assess.

There are other practical implications that statutory services must consider in order to meet their new duties in relation to the two Acts. This includes ensuring that there is access to appropriate information across all age groups, including the needs of young people in transition; the alignment of assessment processes to ensure that responsibilities for both children's services and adult social care are covered; and developing joint commissioning arrangements across the 0–25 age group and specifically commissioning for transition. It has been suggested that commissioners will need to develop the market to better meet the needs of transition, so that young people can use their direct payments and personal budgets to buy appropriate services that promote independence, access to employment, education and training as well as providing a wider range of housing options (Preparing for Adulthood programme 2015). Service providers will need to reflect the quality standards that young people will expect, in addition to being flexible, good value and responsive to their needs. It is anticipated that the advances of technology and information technology (IT) will present challenges for providers in relation to marketing and delivering their services, as young people become increasingly skilled and adept at using social networking and online marketplace systems.

Local authorities will need to become more skilled at projecting and anticipating the needs of young people in transition in order to ensure appropriate resources are allocated to assessment and support planning. Indeed, Broadhurst *et al.* (2012) argue that successful transition can only be achieved through good financial planning. This should not only be a responsibility for adult social care, but requires planning and commitment from education, employment, housing and health services in order to effectively project future needs arising from transition. As Broadhurst *et al.* (2012, p.126) indicate, there is a clear need for 'informed analysis and systematic monitoring of transition needs' across the relevant agencies. Indeed, through the early identification of young people and tracking their multiple transitions, statutory services should be in a position to project young people's needs; assess, plan and review any support they need; and project the likely resource implications for any services needed. As such, the pathway should be developed in such a way that young people are not 'missed' and where there are no *surprises*. It is not only in the best interests of the young person and their family to make sure that this happens, but it should also be a priority for service providers and commissioners.

The integrated and coordinated approach anticipated through the implementation of EHC plans is likely to support this process. The increased pooling of budgets and jointly funded packages of care are also anticipated outcomes of the reform programme, and will require greater recognition of the needs of young people in transition across all agencies within a culture of strategic planning, risk-sharing and pooled resources. Indeed, Merriman (2009, p.6) suggests that effective engagement across agencies is a 'key tool in ensuring a smooth transition for disabled young people'. She advocates that effective information-sharing about individual young people will ensure that commissioning is led by the needs and aspirations of young people as well as planning based on early identification of young people and the coordination of assessments.

A number of strategies have been adopted at a local level to support multi-agency strategy and planning for transition within localities. This includes the development of clear, strategic, multi-agency protocols to set out the vision for transition and the priorities and responsibilities of each agency. Such protocols require senior level sign-up, and should be developed in partnership across agencies, involving young people and their representatives in order to ensure that the protocol is relevant and effective (Merriman 2009). Best practice suggests that the protocol and pathway should also be overseen by and its application monitored through a multi-agency steering group to provide effective governance, and again, should involve young people and their families.

As has been seen, the participation of young people and their families, at a strategic, service and individual level, is essential. Involvement has to be meaningful, and should be seen as an 'empowering process' that requires systems change to allow young people to take control of their own transition. Access to high-quality information, advice and guidance is also seen as a key component to successful transition (Merriman 2009).

As set out earlier in this chapter, the transition process is dynamic, multi-faceted and needs to respond to changing circumstances, needs and aspirations. It is clear that the regular monitoring and review of transition plans is built into this process in order to ensure that they are continuing to deliver the aspirations of young people. Regular monitoring and review will need to form part of local arrangements for EHC plans, and how agencies plan to deliver their new responsibilities within this evolving context.

CONCLUSION

This chapter has set out the critical importance of the transition from school to adulthood for young people with disabilities and their families. It has also illustrated the significance for those agencies working with young people in transition to ensure effective arrangements in order to fulfil their statutory responsibilities as well as supporting young people to fulfil their potential and in ensuring efficient use of resources. The chapter has highlighted the prominence of person-centred approaches, multi-agency working, coordinated and timely assessments, and the provision of information, advice and guidance as being key ingredients to achieving successful transitions. The importance of involving young people to develop their own transition plans and supporting families to fully participate is also a major driver, set out in recent policy and legislation that underpins transition.

However, we have seen that practice and implementation have continued to be variable and disjointed, with many local areas struggling to deliver successful transition arrangements. Too often, transition continues to be rushed, service-driven and risk-averse, resulting in missed opportunities for young people and their families, alongside costly and restrictive service provision. Communication between agencies and with young people and their families has also proven to be poor, resulting in unnecessary conflict, confusion and anxiety.

The changing legal context against which transition will be delivered has an opportunity to address some of these challenges. However, there needs to be recognition that to do this effectively will require buy-in from young people, their families, professionals and agencies in order to ensure that young people with disabilities have the chance to have the same opportunities offered to them as their non-disabled peers. This will require opportunities to be stimulated and developed in relation to the outcomes that young people want to achieve. This must include access to education, employment and training; having choice, control and flexibility over any services they use; being able to live healthy lives and having access to responsive health services; availability of a range of housing options in local communities; good transport provision, including independent travel training; feeling a sense of safety and security; access to youth, recreation and leisure services; and having personal relationships – indeed, all of the outcomes that young people frequently indicate that are important to them and are well documented throughout the research.

As such, the next few years will be significant to see whether this changing context will be able to deliver the outcome focus and person-centred approach promised within the new legal framework and so critically needed in order to achieve successful transition for young people with disabilities. This is a stressful, uncertain and challenging time for young people and their families. Therefore transition practice on the ground must reflect more than the rhetoric of legislation, policy and process if it is going to support young people to truly achieve their potential.

2

TRANSITIONS AND SPECIAL EDUCATIONAL NEEDS

INTRODUCTION

Choosing our future career and education pathway is taken for granted in the non-disabled population. Education is a prime focus within adolescence, and forms an integral part of a young person's life. For young people with disabilities, however, educational choices can be restricted, both in terms of physical barriers as well as assumptions about disability and ability.

This chapter aims to guide practitioners through the education transition planning for young people with disabilities, to establish what the legal requirements are, to identify key roles and to give some useful practical examples about the education system. Education policy and practice is in a significant period of change at present, with the introduction of the Children and Families Act 2014. It is essential that those supporting young people with disabilities have a good understanding of how these changes could affect young people with disabilities, and that they establish ways to support them effectively. In order to do this, practitioners will need to understand what was in place prior to the Children and Families Act 2014, as the coming months and years will see a transition in education, transferring from a special educational needs (SEN) process to the EHC plan.

OVERVIEW OF POLICY AND LEGISLATION

Under the Education Act 1944, those with disabilities were categorised under labels such as 'uneducatable' or 'educationally sub-normal'. However, the 1987 Warnock report (Committee of Enquiry into the Education of Handicapped Children and Young People 1978), followed by the Education Act 1981, brought about radical changes in education for those with SEN, and a key theme in the report was the need for an inclusive approach to education that focused on common educational goals for all children, regardless of their disabilities. The report identified that children with disabilities could be educated in mainstream schools where it was felt appropriate, and that all schools should have an identified SEN teacher. The Education Act 1981 introduced Statements of SEN, a significant feature in education for those with disabilities that has continued to be reviewed, analysed and developed within legislation. The Act imposed duties on local authorities to make a statutory assessment of children with SEN or complex disabilities in order to establish what specific support they would need throughout their education. Statements were designed to encourage, where possible, the education of those with disabilities in mainstream schools, provided that this was compatible with the provision of well-organised education for the other children being educated and the efficient use of resources (Dare and O'Donovan 2002).

In 1994 the government produced a SEN Code of Practice (DFE 1944), which introduced the need for special educational needs coordinators (SENCOs) in all schools. Since then, several reports have strengthened the need for SENCOs, including *Every Child Matters* (DfES 2003) and *Removing Barriers to Achievement* (DfES 2004). The Education Act 1996 sought to consolidate all previous education legislation, and further detailed the need for SENCOs, and for children with SEN to be integrated where possible within mainstream institutions.

There are, however, far too many reports and pieces of legislation that cover SEN, and it would warrant a whole chapter to do it justice, but listed below are some of the more important ones:

- *Excellence for All Children: Meeting Special Educational Needs* (DfEE 1997).

- The Special Educational Needs and Disability Act 2001 followed on from the Disability Discrimination Act 1995, and made provisions to ensure that children with disabilities were not discriminated against within educational settings.

- Education (Special Educational Needs) (England) (Consolidation) Regulations 2000.

- Education and Inspections Act 2006.

- Learning and Skills Act 2000.

WHAT IS A STATEMENT OF SEN?

A Statement of SEN is an official document detailing a child's learning difficulties and the help and resources needed to ensure the child can continue to make educational progress. At present, this is what most young people with a disability will have to document their education needs, although it is soon to be replaced by the EHC plan (explored in greater detail later in this chapter). The statementing process begins with a statutory assessment, which is the method used by a local authority to identify a child's SEN, and to decide what provision to make for the child (Power 2010). The assessment should take into account the views of the child, parents, school, educational psychologist and when appropriate, social services.

Where the assessment concludes that a Statement is required because a child has a disability or learning difficulty, the local authority has a responsibility to include a description of the child's difficulties and learning objectives, and how it is envisaged that these will be achieved. Specifically, the Statement should address an establishment for the child to receive schooling, any additional resources, for example, speech and language support that is required, and a detailed description of how the child's educational and non-educational needs will be met within that establishment. Statements are required to be reviewed annually at the beginning of each academic year, and can be amended if necessary. As part of the annual review process the school is required to complete an Individual Education Plan (IEP). This communicates the targets to be met and the anticipated outcomes to all involved in its delivery (Tod, Castles and Blamires 1998). At each annual review the targets are reviewed and new ones set accordingly.

There has been widespread criticism of the effectiveness of Statements, their generation of an oppressive weight of administration and paperwork (Gross 2013), and the SEN framework, leading to radical reforms. Parents and carers have long struggled with the complexities of SEN services, and the local Parent Partnership Service offers support to parents struggling to navigate the system. Parent Partnerships now exist in all authorities to give parents of children with SEN support and advice through trained volunteers known as 'independent parent advisers' (Halliwell 2003). The role of the Parent Partnership is likely to become more prominent during the move from Statements to EHC plans, as parents will undoubtedly seek advice around what the changes may mean for their child.

THE FUTURE IN RELATION TO EHC PLANS

At the time of writing (2014), the whole landscape of SEN is undergoing radical reform, and the Children and Families Act 2014 is now in force. One of the most significant outcomes of the Act is the EHC plan replacing the existing Statement of SEN. It is intended to be a single assessment and planning process that spans 0–25 years for young people with SEN, offering a personalised approach, and allowing young people and their parents to have a greater level of control. It was phased in in September 2014, and replaces a need for a Section 139A when looking at post-school options. Essentially, the plans have the same legal requirements as a Statement, but should be more outcome-focused and dedicated to meeting the aspirations of the young person. EHC plans should not only focus on the needs of the young person, but should also include their aspirations and wishes for the future. Reviews of the plan should be focused on their progress towards life outcomes across education, health, employment and an independent life (DfE 2011). Examples of outcomes could include securing alternative accommodation, accessing meaningful daytime activity, gaining employment, volunteering, or going on to a local or residential college.

KEY FEATURES OF AN EHC PLAN IN RELATION TO TRANSITION

- It remains in place until the outcomes of the plan are achieved, or until the young person turns 25.

- It should name an educational institution that is the preference of the parents and young person.

- Social services should be included within the plan if a child is legally entitled to receive social care.

- Young people should have the opportunity to have an individual budget.

- EHC plans must include provision to assist in preparation for adulthood from Year 9 onwards.

A requirement of the Children and Families Act 2014 is for each local authority to publish a Local Offer. In short, this should be compiled in consultation with young people and their families to set out what is available within the county to support young people with SEN. Publication of this information is required to be easily accessible to young people and their parents to help them make informed choices about their future. Franklin and Sanderson (2014) suggest that it is important to provide families with information of what is possible, and not just what is available, stressing the importance of being person-centred and not fixed on what services currently exist. The Local Offer will tell the young people what help they can get with their healthcare, and what help they can get from social care services, as well as what help they can get with their education (DFE 2014). In addition, it should include information about transport to and from educational establishments, arrangements for moving out of home, support that can be accessed when learning elsewhere in the county, and what support there is for entering adulthood and finding training/work.

In order to effectively cover plans for education up to the age of 25, EHC plans need to have active involvement from all areas of a young person's life. The SEN Code of Practice suggests that plans should be person-cantered and that the objectives are SMART:

- Specific: they should specify what you want to achieve and how.

- Measurable: it should be possible to measure if you are achieving your goals.

- Achievable: outcomes should be achievable, both in terms of ability and resources.

- Realistic: is it realistic that the outcome can be achieved?

- Time: a timescale should be given to indicate how long it is likely to take to achieve each outcome.

SMART outcomes are rooted in management theories and have been used for many years in the management field. Their popularity is growing in health and social care, and can provide the writer of care and support plans with a consistent framework to follow. Both the Children and Families Act 2014 and the Care Act 2014 make reference to the use of SMART objectives, and it is worthwhile for transition workers to familiarise themselves with the concept, or to attend a training session.

TRANSITION PRACTITIONER TIPS

- Investigate what training sessions or information sessions there are in your local authority around EHC plans.

- Get involved in EHC pilots if there is time, or consider ways you can input into the EHC plan working groups.

The very nature of the EHC plan is to ensure that the young person remains central to the planning process, and that education, health and social care all work together in meeting the needs of the young person. While everyone working in these services would agree with that sentiment, we have yet to see how this may work in practice, as each service continues to have its own budget and processes to work to. The real challenge is to achieve a response which is 'doubly holistic' – that is, it provides continuity for the child over time, but at any point achieves an integrated approach by all services to the child and family (Franklin and Sanderson 2014). There is essentially a real opportunity here to coordinate support for young people, and to make the whole process of transition more joined-up. Having a planning meeting to transfer/complete a new EHC plan is critical to making it effective.

YEAR 9 REVIEW

The Year 9 review continues to be seen as a pivotal point and the start of the transition process for young people with disabilities. The Connexions service, established in the 1990s, was developed to offer careers advice and guidance to all young people aged between 13 and 19, and for young people with disabilities up to the age of 25. Connexions personal advisers (PAs) had a legal duty, under the Department for Education and Skills' SEN Code of Practice 2001, to attend all Year 9 and Year 11 reviews, and responsibility to develop and coordinate a transition plan. Availability of Connexions PAs has reduced following the 2008 economic recession, as budget cuts within local authorities have forced many Connexions offices to close. Despite this, the local authority continues to have responsibility for sending a targeted support worker to fulfil this role.

The effectiveness of a Year 9 transition review can vary from school and area, but it is crucial that young people are prepared for and have time to consider their contribution to such a review. Good practice dictates that person-centred approaches should be used in all reviews; however, it could be argued that for this review, it is essential. This review and plan form the basis for planning out the life of the young person, and if it did not represent their needs, wants and wishes, this would be completely inappropriate. Attendance at the school review by all potential funding authorities will support realistic outcome setting, and help to manage the expectations of the young people and their carers. Ideally, a young person and their family will be informed about their indicative resource allocation before their Year 10 person-centred review. The Year 10 review can therefore trigger the formation of a support plan, which will be developed and then agreed as the young person leaves school with their personal budget (DH 2010). In reality, few local authorities achieve an assessment and indicative budget earlier than the age of 17, which can result in the support planning process being rushed. Using the Resource Allocation System (RAS) appropriately should enable local authorities to be more proactive, although it is possible that funding panels may not agree confirmed funding until the support plan is complete. Further information around personal budgets and Resource Allocation Systems can be found in Chapter 4.

Although the review to plan the transition is still largely referred to as the Year 9 review, it could actually take place at any point during the young person's secondary education. For young people and families, the earlier they can plan, the better. Much of the literature around transition suggests that it is never too early to plan, and earlier planning helps with a clear focus and direction. Some families, however, may find the process stressful, particularly as services, resources, policy and legislation are all likely to have changed significantly in the final four years before the young person leaves school. Reviews are always arranged and organised by the school, and head teachers have a responsibility for inviting partner agencies that they feel need to contribute to it. Reviews of EHC plans are likely to require a longer time slot than that of previous education-only annual reviews. Allowing adequate time for all elements of the EHC plan to be fully reviewed in a person-centred manner is fundamental to the success of the plan for the young person.

Preparation for the review should begin in the classroom, where teaching staff and teaching assistants prepare the young person for the review. Although the process starts with school, however, they sometimes only focus on education rather than the bigger picture (Franklin and Sanderson 2014). Planning for the review should begin by establishing if the young person can attend their review.

Person-centred transition planning should not be seen as an 'add-on'; rather, it should be an integral part of people's everyday lives (Sanderson, Sholl and Jordan n.d.). It is good practice that wherever possible the young person should attend the review; however, there are likely to be circumstances due to behaviour, communication difficulties or health needs where this is just not possible, although it doesn't prevent the young person's contribution being gathered in other ways.

CASE STUDY – BETH

Beth is a 16-year-old young woman with severe physical and learning disabilities. She has limited communication, although she can use 'yes' and 'no' signs reliably to closed questions. Her responses can take some time to give, and she gets particularly tired after lunch. Beth has a good relationship with her teacher who has been working with her for the past eight months.

Consider:

- Who is best placed to get Beth's feedback?

- How could Beth's likes and dislikes be identified?

- How can Beth's wishes for the future be identified?

- What resources/equipment could support Beth to take an active role in the review?

Beth's school is a special school for those with physical and learning disabilities, and it takes a proactive approach to planning with the

32

young people it supports. The school has developed a set of questions/ review format that can be adapted and changed to suit the needs of each young person. For Beth, a time slot was identified within her timetable to focus weekly on transition planning. This included filming her undertaking activities that she enjoys, and her undertaking specific educational targets. In addition, it involved the school developing a set of closed questions only requiring 'yes' or 'no' answers personal to her that enabled them to check and verify the information, for example: 'Do you like the food at school?' In response to this question, Beth was able to answer 'no'. Over the weeks, staff would alter the way in which the question was asked, for example, 'Is the food at school bad?', and again Beth was able to indicate 'yes'. During the review Beth's video clips were shown, and she was again asked the questions listed, and to give her response and contribution.

What this case study demonstrates is that no matter how severe the young person's impairment, they will be able to contribute in a meaningful way if they receive appropriate assistance (Warner 2006), and this should always be the basis for beginning each review. There is also significant evidence that planning and preparation for the review is best done within the class environment. Realistically, however, caseload pressures and the work demands of transition workers may prevent them from undertaking lengthy work with the young people to gain their views for transition planning, although there may be ways in which they can maximise a young person's contribution.

TRANSITION PRACTITIONER TIPS

- Connect with schools: ideally it would be preferable to have a link school with which you work, where you can build relationships with teaching staff, and establish what role the school will play.

- Ask schools: although it wouldn't be advisable to tell schools how to do their jobs, gently reminding them of the benefits of preparing for transition reviews in advance is a good idea. Look at examples in other authorities, and suggest that schools continue to adapt these.

- Consider resources: look at the resources that can help to gather student views. The Transition Pathway's Big Picture could easily be adapted and used by schools in their timetable. The Big Picture is an information pack aimed at young people with disabilities and provides accessible information about the transition process. Informing young people of their rights and preparing them in advance will support them in making a valuable contribution. Similarly, one-page profiles can help young people to think about what's important to them, rather than focusing on the views of the parents or carers.

- What can you do? Pressures and workload can be heavy and it may be hard to invest time. Look at ways you can gain the views of the young people prior to review – could you facilitate a group where young people could discuss their views?

- Provide information: is there accessible information for young people and families about post-school options? Is there a resource file kept in your office, or a website that young people and carers can access? Most young people want advice and guidance, and particularly in early planning, just pointing them in the right direction to access appropriate information may assist in managing their anxieties.

- Encourage person-centred planning: encourage the young people to investigate post-school options.

Used appropriately, the transition plan and annual review process can be the most effective form of transition planning, but it will only be so if all agencies sign up to attending and implementing it.

POST-18 EDUCATION

Historically, young people with disabilities have been entitled to remain within school education until the age of 19, but many special schools have now reduced this to 18, in line with the Education and Skills Act 2008 enforcement that by 2015, all young people in England will need to remain in education or training up to the age of 18. Leaving the relative safety and familiarity of the special school environment can provoke feelings of fear and anxiety in young people and their family. The school has often provided a consistent amount of support for many years, and considering alternative provision may be difficult for the young people.

Parents in particular may have pre-conceived ideas about local college provision. They may not be aware that local colleges are able to offer courses for people with disabilities, or be worried about the level of support they are able to offer. Many special schools offer 'link courses' to local further education colleges that involve young people undertaking particular subjects, such as cooking, within the college environment. This is beneficial in not only introducing young people to the college environment, but also for dispelling some of the myths around support that parents may have. The advantages of attending a local college are significant. There is the opportunity for a transition to take place between the school and the college, ensuring that anxiety of change is kept to a minimum.

ADVANTAGES AND DISADVANTAGES OF ATTENDING LOCAL COLLEGE

- Local college courses, although advertised as full-time courses, may actually only offer three to four days per week, or half-days. This can pose a significant problem for families who are used to the five days provided by school, and who may have work or other employment commitments to consider.

- Transport and access to college can be a major factor. The education department will usually assist with transport, but only if this is to the nearest local college, meaning that those with disabilities may struggle to do a course they enjoy or that has more days because it is at a college on the other side of the county.

- By attending a local college, young people maintain existing friendships and build genuine links by accessing their local community.

- Local colleges are unlikely to offer the young person the opportunity to live away from family and undertake a 24-hour curriculum that focuses not only on academic education, but also on improving independence and life skills.

35

Local colleges have worked hard to improve access to their courses over recent years, and most further education colleges also offer specific programmes for people with learning disabilities, which include specialist help (Gabbitas Education 2005). Yet there continues to be a group of young people whose needs cannot be adequately met within local college provision, prompting young people and families to look at alternative specialist college provision that is frequently out of the county.

USE OF RESIDENTIAL COLLEGES

Sections 139A–139C of the Learning and Skills Act 2000 stated that the local authority must conduct an assessment of learners with disabilities if it believes that the person will leave school, at the end of the last year of compulsory schooling, to receive post-16 education or training or higher education. Under the 2000 Act the Learning and Skills Council (LSC) was responsible for securing the provision of facilities for post-16 education and training in England. Previously, Section 139A learning difficulties assessments were completed by Connexions PAs who had attended the young person's reviews, working closely with the young person, parents, school and other involved agencies to establish needs. A Section 139A assessment needed to be completed for young people looking to go to local or residential college, allowing the allocation of the correct level of funding from the relevant agencies to be secured.

For many years, Connexions PAs had no accountability to funding agencies, and were seen as the link between the young person, their aspirations and needs, their family, education and support services, acting as advocate and broker (Dee 2006). This led to some criticism in relation to the Section 139A assessment, including concerns that it was driven by choice rather than individual need. Essentially Connexions PAs presented the wishes of the young people and their parents when recommending that a local college could not meet the young person's needs, rather than actually establishing a need for alternative provision. It could be argued that this was a person-centred approach to planning; however, it inevitably led to the purchasing of high-cost residential college placements, and young people accessing education away from their local area. This, in turn, had repercussions for local college provision, arguing that they were unable to increase their courses locally as money was being diverted out of the area, prompting local authorities to establish that a local college placement could not meet the young person's needs before considering a residential college. Given the need to tighten resources with the recent budget cuts, and the introduction of the Children and Families Act 2014, there is the potential for access to specialist colleges to get more difficult. Murray (2012) argues that placing young people who would benefit from specialist further education in local colleges or training providers may help local authorities make short-term savings, but in the long term it could prove more costly.

It is likely, however, that there will continue to be a group of young people whose needs cannot be met in local college provision, and for whom a specialist college is most appropriate. Going to a specialist college can provide access to specialist equipment, support and teaching that a local college may be unable to provide (Gabbitas Education 2013), and give young people valuable experiences of staying away from home and improving their independence skills.

Many specialist colleges offer residential placements for 38 weeks a year, and have a high profile at transition events and conferences. They say that the residential element is key to their holistic approach that builds an individual's confidence and equips them with social skills after perhaps a lifetime of isolation and inactivity (Brindle 2013). This, alongside the experience of other young people who have left school, and accessible information provided by COPE (see Foxwell 2010) and the Association of National Specialist Colleges (Natspec), can make these colleges an attractive option for young people and their parents who, in some cases, may see this as their route into independent living.

CASE STUDY – GRACE

Grace is a young woman with moderate learning disabilities and autistic spectrum disorder (ASD). She has completed a course at a specialist local college, and has identified that she would like to gain employment in catering and hospitality. She has gained some skills in this area, and has looked at local college courses that may offer her additional skills and prepare her for open employment. Many of these courses, however, are not able to cater for her ASD and anxiety issues. Therefore, she and her parents have identified a residential college that functions as a hotel and offers on-site education in her preferred course area, as well as enabling her to gain employability skills.

In order to access this college, Grace required agreement from the Education Funding Agency (EFA) to fund the placement. The EFA argued that some of its placement was social care-related, and therefore asked for a contribution from adult social care. It is acknowledged that the primary reason for Grace accessing a residential college is to receive education/training to improve her employability. Therefore the education representative took a lead in compiling the EHC plan. The social care worker had input into the plan by lifting information from the personal care assessment and populating the social care section of the EHC plan.

In this situation, the social care worker and education representative completed an EHC plan. In order to provide an indicative personal budget from social care, the transition worker was required to complete a personal care assessment under the National Health Service (NHS) and Community Care Act 1990, and to follow existing processes within social services. This included completing the budget calculator created by the Resource Allocation System (RAS), and completing a funding request. Following agreement of an indicative budget at the Resource Allocation Panel, the education representative was able to consider what was included in the Local Offer around education, and factor in all costs associated with providing support and education locally. This included:

- cost of local college provision per year

- cost of transport to and from the college placement

- cost of supported accommodation/social care needs (social care indicative budget)

- additional costs of specialised health support such as physiotherapy, speech and language therapy and occupational therapy.

Undertaking this type of service and cost analysis enabled the EFA to make a decision about whether to offer a residential college placement, and to complete an EHC plan.

TRANSITION PRACTITIONER TIPS

- Find out about courses offered in your Local Offer, and who is responsible in your area for making applications to the EFA. It is a good idea to form professional relationships with these representatives, whether they are Connexions PAs or other local authority agents.

- Ask the agents what the process is for applying to residential colleges, what their processes are for making decisions, and when a decision is likely to be confirmed. Transition planning will often depend on where the young person is going for education, and if decisions about residential college are not made early enough, this will have an impact on the plan that can be put in place locally at short notice.

Maintaining contact with young people who are likely to require adult social care services while they are away at college is an essential part of transition planning. Often, the biggest argument made for a young person to access a residential college is to develop their independence skills and equip them for supported living in the future. It is therefore natural for young people and their parents to want them to move on to their own accommodation and support arrangements when they leave home, as it is possible that they will lose the skills they have gained if they were to return home to live with their family. In order to support these wishes appropriately, transition workers need to monitor the young people's needs and maintain contact while they are at residential college. This includes attending annual reviews where they are able to, and re-assessing their needs well in advance of them leaving college. It is worth considering whether the young person can take part in social activities or work experience when they return home during the college holidays to maintain links in their local area.

TRANSITION WORKER TIPS

- Ensure contact is maintained with young people away at residential college by attending reviews and visiting during college holidays.

- Consider support needs at home during the college holidays. Do family members work? Is additional support required at this time? Is there a personal budget or other available voluntary resources or funding that could be used for holiday activities that promote maintenance of community links?

- Ensure that a re-assessment of the young person's need post-college is completed as early as possible, particularly if alternative accommodation is required at this point.

CONCLUSION

This chapter outlines the changes in special educational needs provision over recent years and the impact this is having on educational choices for young people with disabilities. The radical changes currently taking place in SEN services will undoubtedly change the landscape of specialist education provision and reinforce the need for a strategic approach to transition planning. Developing a multi-agency transition pathway that utilises person- centred approaches should be high on the agenda for councils if they are to adhere to the Children and Families Act (2014) intention that services need to be more joined up and consider holistically the needs of the young person. Successfully embedoding a transition pathway will take more than senior management devising a written protocol. It involves all agencies committing to this way of working, changing some of their internal processes and ensuring that attendance at the transition/ EHC plan review is a priority.

This chapter has recognised that EHC plans are in their infancy and it has yet to be ascertained if they will do as is intended and replace some of our cumbersome and bureaucratic processes with a single, holistic and comprehensive plan for children with the most complex needs (Franklin and Sanderson 2014).

Developing close working relationships with schools, health partners and the education authority can support transitions workers to plan holistically with young people, however, as identified throughout this chapter, there remains a significant challenge to all practitioners supporting the young person to ensure that they have appropriate access to information around post-school educational opportunities and that their needs and wishes are appropriately represented.

RESOURCES

For information on Parent Partnerships, see the Information, Advice & Support Services Network: *www.iassnetwork.org.uk.*

For information on the SEN reforms, EHC plan and SEN processes, see the Preparing for Adulthood programme website: *www.preparingforadulthood.org.uk/resources/pfa-resources/ehc-plans-and-assessment-process.*

For information on Individual Education Plans, see: *www.individualeducationplans.com.*

For information on the Transition Pathway and the Big Picture, see: *centreofexcellence.etsb.qc.ca/files/2014/09/The-Big-Picture.pdf.*

For information around transition planning/person-centred planning and support planning, see: *www.helensandersonassociates.co.uk.*

For information on the Preparing for Adulthood programme, see: *www.preparingforadulthood. org.uk.*

For information around specialist residential colleges, see the Association of National Specialist Colleges website: *www.natspec.org.uk.*

For information on one-page profiles, see the Helen Sanderson Associates website: *www.helensandersonassociates.co.uk.*

DfE (Department for Education) (2014) *Special Educational Needs and Disability Code of Practice: 0 to 25 Years Statutory Guidance for Organisations who Work with and Support Children and Young People with Special Educational Needs and Disabilities.* London: The Stationery Office.

DH (Department of Health) (2008) *A Transition Guide for All Services: Key Information for Professionals about the Transition Process for Disabled Young People.* London: The Stationery Office. Available at www.transitioninfonetwork.org.uk/resources/policy-guidance/a-transition-guide-for-all-services.aspx.

DH (2010) *Person-Centred Planning Advice for Using Person-Centred Thinking: Planning and Reviews in Schools and Transition.* London: The Stationery Office. Available at www.ndti.org.uk/uploads/files/PCP_in_schools_and_transitions.pdf.

3

TRANSITIONS AND CHILDREN'S SERVICES

INTRODUCTION

Local authorities generally accept that transition between children's and adults services should begin around the age of 14 when schools have a legal requirement under the Education Act 1996 to hold a transition review. The Care Act 2014 echoes the need for earlier planning, indicating that children's and adult services have a responsibility to work together to plan effectively for transition to adulthood. There are a variety of resources used within schools to begin to plan for transition, and these are generally used around the age of 16. Although the majority of the literature written around transition defends a need for transition planning to begin at the age of 14, there is an argument that planning too early for transition may be counterproductive, as services, opportunities and circumstances may change considerably by the time the young person reaches 18. Therefore, while it is recognised that it is useful to get key partners thinking about transition planning at 14, active planning may be more appropriate from 16. Obviously this depends on the individual, their needs and circumstances, and in some cases more intense planning is likely to be required. For the purpose of this chapter we consider the legal statuses in children's services, and the impact this may have on the transition process for young people who are 16 or older.

ELIGIBILITY FOR AND ACCESS TO ADULT SERVICES

For young people, family carers and professionals, the process of navigating two separate directorates, sets of legislation and processes can be confusing and problematic. A key problem leading to lack of continuity in provision across transition stems from the different entitlement criteria and definitions between children's and adult services (DCSF and DH 2007). Eligibility criteria for Children with Disabilities Teams are largely dependent on the child being classed as a 'child in need' under the Children Act 1989. (This notion is explored in greater detail later.) However, it is evident that the threshold for receiving services as a child with a disability is much lower than that of adult services, where eligibility is more policy-driven and categorises levels of need. Fair Access to Care Services (FACS) is the framework for assessing the level of need someone may be entitled to in adult services, and ranks those needs from low, moderate, substantial to critical (DH 2003). Given that the majority of local authorities meet only critical or substantial needs, the potential for young people to lose their eligibility for support in adult services is likely.

Definitions of disability can vary from children's to adult services, with the diagnosis of certain conditions not automatically establishing eligibility. People with ASD will not be assessed as having a learning disability, but will be near the borderline, and often miss out due to arbitrary criteria such as a certain level of IQ (Joint Committee on Human Rights 2008a). Early identification of these young people prior to turning 18 can help transition workers to refer to autism/Asperger's specialist teams or other support agencies, and under the Care Act 2014 services still have a duty to provide information and advice, even if a young person is not entitled to support.

CASE STUDY – CHRIS

Chris is a 17-year-old boy with Asperger's syndrome currently seeing a support worker from Barnardo's to help him once a week to access his local community. He has no other learning disability or physical disability, and can now access the community independently. He and his parents would like his current support worker to continue post-18 as he has developed a good relationship with him, and struggles to make friends. However, it has been identified through a screening visit by the transition worker that he is not eligible for support from the transition team as he does not have a significant learning or physical disability. In this case, he was referred to another team who work with vulnerable people for an assessment of his needs. It is likely, however, that he will not be considered to have a critical or substantial need for this support now that he is able to access the community independently. More appropriate ways of him making friends and maintaining relationships may be sought through the use of voluntary support agencies.

TRANSITION PRACTITIONER TIPS

- Familiarise yourself with other local support services and teams that may be able to offer services to vulnerable young people who do not meet adult eligibility criteria.

- Put together an information pack that you can give to young people and families who are unlikely to meet the thresholds for support from adult services. This could include directing young people and their carers to information about the Local Offer.

The introduction of the Care Act 2014 and its seemingly lower thresholds may well address some of the inequity in eligibility criteria across directorates. We will, however, need to wait for the Act to be further embedded in practice before its effectiveness around eligibility can be evaluated further. Families of a child with a disability requesting support will typically be offered support services under the Children Act 1989, and be offered a child in need plan. This makes collecting information and data about young people with disabilities approaching transition easily accessible through Children with Disabilities Teams. Those families who have not asked for support and who have made it through the education system without any social care support sometimes become vulnerable adults in need of support, and have not been identified for transition because they were only in the education system (Joint Committee on Human Rights 2008a). Having previously had the support of school and family, there may not have been a need for a young person with a disability to access services prior to turning 18. There tends to be a significant shift in this as school ends and young people find they need additional support as they approach adulthood. This cohort of young people make up a significant proportion of those approaching transition, and identifying them early on will prevent a need for potentially high-cost packages of support because they have been a 'surprise' to adult services. The Care Act 2014 makes it clear that a young person or their family may ask for an assessment at any point prior to their eighteenth birthday, whether or not they are currently receiving services.

TRANSITION PRACTITIONER TIPS

- Regular quarterly meetings between transition workers/teams and Children with Disabilities Teams can help to improve communication and develop an understanding about the young people entering transition and what their circumstances, needs and current services are. This kind of discussion will also help to identify early on those people who are unlikely to meet adult eligibility criteria, and will allow for prompt signposting to other services.

- Easy read written guidance around eligibility should be provided to young people while they are still in children's services. This could be within an information pack, accessible on websites or given to young people at their 14+ review. There is the potential for this to be included when publishing the local authority's Local Offer.

- The opportunity to meet with young people and screen them against eligibility criteria before their eighteenth birthday is useful. Speak with head teachers, Connexions PAs and so on. to identify any young person who does not access support from children's services currently, but is likely to require support as they reach 18 or leave school.

- Drop-in/surgery sessions at schools can be a useful way of identifying young people in the education system who may not be known to children's services but are likely to require support when they leave school.

- A record/spreadsheet of information collected about all of the young people identified above will help in keeping track of who will require an assessment and who is in need of support. An accurate recording and monitoring system is essential to ensure that you can plan your work, pass on information to other workers, and provide an accurate financial forecast to commissioners and budget holders.

It is fundamental to a good transition that the processes begin within children's services, and that adult services have an understanding of where the young person has come from, what experiences they have had, and the processes and legislation they have been supported under.

OVERVIEW OF LEGISLATION

Support within children's services is governed by the Children Acts 1989 and 2004. One of the key elements of the Children Act 1989 is to place the child at the centre of intervention, and the welfare of the child is paramount. The Children Act 1989 is the legislative spine that provides a foundation for social work with children and young people. It addresses safeguarding issues, and is fundamental in setting out how children's social care should be organised and delivered.

Amendments were made in the 2004 Act, and it was stated in Part 5, Section 3, that authorities need to ascertain the wishes and feelings of the child, and give due consideration to them when assessing the needs of a child under Section 17 of the 1989 Act and in relation to child protection investigations under Section 47. The strategy document, *Every Child Matters: Change for Children* (DfES 2004), brought about a review of the Children Act 1989, amendments of which can be found in the Children Act 2004 (Tassoni *et al.* 2007).

REFERRAL AND ASSESSMENT OF CHILDREN AND YOUNG PEOPLE IN CHILDREN'S SERVICES

Most local authority assessments are based on the *Framework for the Assessment of Children in Need and their Families* (DH, DfEE and Home Office 2000). This provides a basis for enabling professionals to collate, analyse and understand information in order to make judgements and recommendation for support and intervention.

An initial assessment is usually required to establish if a child is in need following referral to children's services. Under the framework, an initial assessment is required to be completed within seven working days of referral, and involves the assessor collating information on the child's developmental needs, the parent's capacity to respond to them, and wider family and environmental factors that may affect them.

The initial assessment will identify if a child or young person is either:

- a child in need (as defined in Section 17 of the Children Act 1989) or

- there is reason to suspect the child/young person is suffering, or is likely to suffer significant harm.

(Section 47, Children Act 1989)

There are a number of possible outcomes from an initial assessment, including an initial plan for support, a more in-depth core assessment, instigation of a child protection enquiry, or emergency action to protect the child. Where no further action from social care is necessary, the child could be referred to integrated services for possible completion of a Common Assessment Framework (CAF).

This can be used in certain circumstances to enable professionals from a variety of services to identify early on the unmet needs of the children, and to work together to meet those needs. While a CAF is not always necessary, as it does not replace the other assessments required under the Children Act, it can be particularly useful for a child with a disability. Teachers, healthcare workers and early years professionals can all take a lead in completing a CAF, and should consider the developmental needs of the child, the views/situation of the parent/carers, and the family environment. The CAF is intended to be introduced at the preventative level, before problems begin to interfere with the child's wellbeing (Asmussen 2011).

Where additional needs are identified through the CAF process, it is likely that a Team Around the Child (TAC) meeting will be held to bring together the child/young person, their carer and all relevant professionals to develop a plan for meeting identified needs. If it becomes clear that one agency has responsibility for meeting the majority of the needs, for example, a child in need of safeguarding, then the child in need process will take over, and the CAF process will be terminated as a result. However, if all agencies involved share equal responsibilities and a coordinated approach is required, an action plan may be created and reviewed regularly in TAC meetings.

Should further investigation of a child or young person's needs be required, progression to a core assessment would be necessary. As with the initial assessment, this should be completed by a qualified professional and based on the *Framework for the Assessment of Children in Need and their Families* (DH *et al.* 2000). A plan to support the child should be developed if it is considered that the child/young person is a child in need.

A significant proportion of young people in transition will have a core assessment and a child in need plan, both of which can be useful tools to gather information at the beginning of the transition planning process.

WHAT IS A 'CHILD IN NEED'?

Section 17 of the Children Act 1989 defines a child as being in need in law if:

- he or she is unlikely to achieve or maintain or to have the opportunity to achieve or maintain a reasonable standard of health or development without provision of services from the local authority

- his or her health or development is likely to be significantly impaired, or further impaired, without the provision of services from the local authority

- he or she has a disability.

The assumption that any child with a disability is a child in needs requires authorities to assess children referred to them and complete a child in need plan. A child in need meeting should take place within 28 days of completion of the assessment.

The purpose of a child in need plan is to establish specific needs and identify ways in which to meet those needs. The plan should be developed in partnership with the child/young person, their parents/carers and other relevant professionals. Any services suggested or implemented should be clearly linked to achieving outcomes and goals for that young person, and will need to have timescales attached in order to accurately measure the success of the intervention/young person's progression. The plan should relate specifically to the areas within the framework and should specifically consider:

- the child's developmental needs around health, education, emotional and behavioural development, identity, family and social relationships, social presentation and self-care skills

- family and environmental factors that may impact on the child and on parenting capacity such as family functioning, family social integration and community resources.

Young people with disabilities and a child in need plan will predominantly live at home with their family, and the plans will focus on how to support them to remain in that family environment. Child in need plans typically identify services or support to enable young people to meet their identified outcomes, and examples of such services include respite/short breaks, outreach support to access the community, homecare and access to play schemes during school holidays.

TRANSITION PRACTITIONER TIPS

- Where possible, attend child in need reviews prior to the young person turning 18 to establish what support is currently in place, and what needs to be continued into adulthood.

- If a young person and their family are accessing respite or support services that end at age 18, consider what could be available in adult services, and find out how to refer to adult services.

- Aim to have the personal assessment under the NHS and Community Care Act completed twelve to six months prior to the young person turning 18. This will support identification of appropriate services and allow funding for a personal budget to be requested.

- Consider developing a plan between the children and adult support providers to facilitate transition. Is it possible for adult services workers to shadow the support offered by children's services? Could the young person begin

> introductory visits to adult provision while still accessing children's provision? This will ensure a smoother transition and prevent a break in support.

Once a child in need plan is in place, as a minimum, child in need review meetings should take place annually. Depending on the complexity of the young person's needs and their circumstances, this may need to be more frequent. For young people with SEN and those with access to residential short breaks, consideration should be given to combining the child in need review with the SEN and short breaks review. This provides a more holistic approach to considering all areas of the young person's life, and reduces the number of meetings the young people, parents/carers and professionals need to attend.

It is crucial that for young people aged 16 and older, a child in need review needs to focus not only on the current situation, changes to the plan and support services, but also that there is a significant emphasis on what the young person is going to need within adult services, and how they can be supported in making a successful transition.

YOUNG PEOPLE UNDER 18 WHO ARE SUBJECT TO CHILD PROTECTION

Occasionally young people will be entering transition already subject to child protection processes. Where an authority receives information at the point of referral, or during an assessment that gives them reason to suspect that the young person may be at risk of suffering or likely to suffer significant harm, or where an Emergency Protection Order (EPO) has been used, the authority is required to initiate Section 47 enquiries, which, in conjunction with any police investigation, begins the child protection process.

If a child is considered to be at significant risk following the initial child protection conference that takes place 15 days after Section 47 enquiries started, a further child protection conference is convened within one month, and the child is placed on the Child Protection Register. The child protection conference should produce an outline child protection plan identifying risk, short- and long-term objectives, and who should do what and when; the core group has responsibility for developing and operationalising the plan as a working tool (Wilson and James 2007).

CHILD PROTECTION PLANS

A child can be considered to require a child protection plan under a number of categories:

- physical abuse

- sexual abuse

- emotional abuse

- neglect

- multiple abuse.

The role of the lead professional, in many cases a social worker from children's services, and in some cases a transition worker in a transition team, is to arrange regular core group meetings and review the plan, monitoring/measuring outcomes. The first meeting of the core group should take place seven days following the child protection conference, and every six weeks from then onwards.

Core groups consist of all those involved in the child's care and, where possible, the child and their family. Important members of a core group may be:

- foster carers

- professionals, doctors, community nurses, teachers, and so on, involved in the case

- representatives from voluntary agencies involved, for example, Barnardo's.

Transition workers have an important role in attending core groups for young people with disabilities, and will need to consider how the identified risks will be managed when the young person turns 18. Where it is considered that these risks will remain into adulthood, work should begin early to assess the capacity of the young person, and consideration given to applications to the Court of Protection should the child need to be looked after away from the family home.

TRANSITION PRACTITIONER TIPS

- Identify why the young person is subject to a child protection plan, and what the risks/potential safeguarding issues are as they enter adulthood.

- Consider early on if the young person has capacity, and how this may impact on managing safeguarding issues as they enter adulthood.

- Do the child and family have legal representation? If so, what are they seeking?

- What are the family and young person's expectations of what will happen at age 18?

- Discuss with the adult protection team/leads and adult legal services any potential safeguarding issues, and seek direction from them.

LOOKED-AFTER CHILDREN

Where it is considered by law that a child can no longer remain in the care of their family, they may become subject to a Care Order (Section 31), an Interim Care Order (Section 38) or an EPO (Section 44, Children Act 1989). In each of these situations children become looked-after without the direct agreement of their parents, although their parents retain parental responsibility.

Some young people will already be subject to a legal plan when they enter transition at 16 or older. Given that they are approaching adulthood at this point, and Care Orders expire on the child's eighteenth birthday, the Children Act is a less appropriate piece of legislation when considering care proceedings for this group. The Mental Capacity Act 2005 applies to young people over the age of 16, and can be useful in providing a legal framework to protect young adults at risk from harm. Where it is considered that a young person lacks capacity and is being put at risk, an application to the Court of Protection can be made to safeguard them from that risk, and, as Brown, Barber and Martin (2008) suggest, the relief to extend beyond the child's eighteenth birthday will no doubt encourage application to the Court of Protection under the Mental Capacity Act rather than using the Children Act.

CASE STUDY – BRETT

Brett is a 17-year-old boy with significant learning and physical disabilities. He lives at home with his father who is a single parent and has been the subject of a Child Protection Plan (CCP) for two years under the category of neglect. There have been ongoing concerns about Brett's poor weight gain, reports he has been left alone, and poor standards of personal hygiene. Brett's father has a history of alcoholism, and despite additional homecare and respite put in place, all professionals feel that there is a significant risk to Brett's health and wellbeing if he remains living with his father.

Brett is consulted about the situation, and his capacity is assessed by a medical professional who considers him to lack capacity about deciding where he wishes to live and the seriousness of his current home situation. Children's services consult with their legal team, and agree to make an application to the Court of Protection for Brett to reside at a short breaks unit in order for his health and weight to be fully assessed. An order is agreed by the Court for a three-month period in which an independent mental capacity advocate (IMCA) is appointed to consult Brett on his views for support post-18.

VOLUNTARY LOOKED-AFTER CHILDREN

In some cases parents become unable to care for a child due to their behaviour, disability or changing medical needs. In such cases, the local authority has a duty to provide accommodation for these young people in agreement with or at the request of their parents. This accommodation can be provided for either short-term or long-term periods, usually in foster care or residential care. This provision is made under Section 20 of the Children Act 1989, and there are no court proceedings involved. When a child becomes looked-after under Section 20, the parents retain full parental responsibility.

The majority of young people with disabilities in transition who are looked-after will be so as a result of Section 20. Their level of disability and complex needs can result in the need for alternative accommodation that can be provided in a variety of ways. Looked-after children accommodated for over 13 weeks should have a pathway plan under the Children Act 1989. These plans should be provided irrespective of other services being provided as a result of disability (DFE 2010). Development of the plan should begin as a young person's support needs are assessed and care plans are created. It should be a live document that is built on the dreams and aspirations of the young person, and supports them to identify the support they need to make a successful transition to adulthood. The Children (Leaving Care) Act 2000 identified that young people leaving care are likely to find the transition to independence hard. The pathway plan is for children aged over 16 and becomes the care plan for the young person when they leave care (Tomlinson and Philpot 2008).

RESIDENTIAL CARE

There is evidence that children with disabilities are more likely to be looked-after, remain in care for longer, and have a higher risk of being placed inappropriately in comparison to children without disabilities (Baker 2011), and given the very complex nature of some of their needs, foster care may not be considered appropriate. Specialist residential care placements for young people under Section 20 can be in the form of a children's home designed to meet the needs of children with disabilities. These are frequently attached to local school sites, and are run and commissioned by the local authority. For other young people with complex physical and learning disabilities, there may not be appropriate education provision locally to meet their needs, and they may require a residential school instead.

CASE STUDY – ARCHIE

Archie is 17 years old and has ASD, challenging behaviour and severe learning disabilities. At around 14 years old his behaviour became too difficult at home for his parents to manage, and he began attacking his siblings. A residential school was found to accommodate him and meet his educational needs, but this was over two hours away from the family home. Archie's parents want him to move closer to the family home when his education finishes at the age of 18.

Planning Archie's transition was problematic for a number of reasons:

- There were few local providers skilled enough to manage Archie's complex needs.

- It was difficult to spend enough time observing Archie at school because of the distance of the placement, to gain robust information to complete the personal assessment.

- Archie was not known to local health services, and links with health professionals proved difficult.

- Once a provider was identified, transition to the new service was hindered by distance and took longer than expected, meaning that Archie remained in the placement past his eighteenth birthday.

- Archie's placement at the school was very expensive in relation to the indicative budget identified through the RAS in adult services, and there was increased pressure from adult social care to move Archie as quickly as possible.

Residential schools are often placed out of county and some distance from the young person's family, and previous research suggests the transition of young people with disabilities leaving residential school placements can be even more problematic than the transition of young people with disabilities living with their families and attending local schools (Beresford and Cavet 2009). For transition workers who have responsibility for young people from the age of 16, they will be required to conduct statutory visits to the residential school on a regular basis. In the first year of the young person's placement they should visit every six weeks. However, if the child has been there for some time, and it is anticipated that they will remain there until their eighteenth birthday, from then on visits should take place every three months.

MAKING STATUTORY VISITS

The purpose of a statutory visit is to ensure that the placement continues to promote the child's welfare, gives the child the opportunity to express their views and wishes, and ensures that care plans are being fully adhered to. There must be an accurate recording of the visit that clearly states:

- who was seen

- whether the child was seen, and if not, why not

- whether the child was seen alone

- any comments made by the child, carers or staff members

- any concerns or difficulties

- observations on the child's welfare/success of the placement

- any requirements for action.

While statutory visits remain a key part of the looked-after children recording process, transition workers will also need to use these visits as a beneficial opportunity to begin transition planning.

ROLE OF THE INDEPENDENT REVIEWING OFFICER

It is a legal requirement under Section 118 of the Adoption and Children Act 2002 that an independent reviewing officer (IRO) is appointed to every looked-after child. Their role is to ensure that the wishes of the child are fully considered, and to quality assure the care planning process. IROs are responsible for monitoring the local authority's review of the care plan, with the aim of ensuring that actions required to implement the care plan are carried out and outcomes monitored (Boylan and Dalrymple 2009). IROs take part in each review for the child, usually chairing each meeting, and making recommendations for the next review.

As part of their duties, IROs need to establish that the social worker is completing regular statutory visits and regular assessments with the young person, ensuring that they remain central to the current placement arrangements and future planning. Those workers with case responsibility from 18+ will need to complete regular statutory visits in addition to an updated social worker looked-after children report, a health assessment and personal education plan.

Transition workers who do not have case responsibility until 18 will need to have an active role in looked-after children reviews, to gather information about the young person, consult them on their views and make plans for post-18 provision.

TRANSITION PRACTITIONER TIPS

- Consider person-centred planning tools that could be used with the young person in preparation for them leaving care.

- Establish an actual placement end date. Although a young person may cease to be classified as a looked-after child at 18, they may be able to remain in the placement to facilitate a period of transition. Knowing the actual placement end date and possibility of staying on post-18 will make identification of post-18 placements easier.

- Find out what support the young person may be entitled to when they leave care, for example, leaving care grants.

YOUNG PEOPLE IN FOSTER CARE

Living with a family is always considered to be preferential to residential care where this can be offered, and the experience of stable family life, and the attention and interest of caring adults who are consistent and special to the child, has been recognised as better than group care (Jones 2011). For young people with disabilities this offers increased stability and the opportunity to have a home life, particularly as adoption may be harder to achieve, resulting in foster placements being more long-term, and significant relationships developing between the foster carer and young person. As with the Court Order or looked-after child status, foster care will come to an end when the young person turns 18, and as a result they are likely to require significant support in preparation for this, particularly if the foster carers do not wish to continue to offer support into adulthood. In these cases, early assessment to establish a young person's needs and aspirations for future accommodation is imperative, in addition to early identification of a personal budget to consider housing options detailed later in Chapter 6.

A move out of long-term foster care is likely to be a significant loss for the young person involved, and consideration should be given to how that loss can be managed, and how they can maintain contact with their foster carers.

Foster carers may be willing to consider continuing to care for the young person post-18. This, in itself, can create a number of issues, although it is generally accepted to be a better option for the young person. It can be supported in a variety of ways, and these should be contemplated when considering a person's capacity to decide where they wish to live. Where the young person has capacity to decide where they want to live and chooses to remain with their foster carers, this could be under a Shared Lives scheme, or as a tenant of the foster carer and accessing a direct payment for support. Where a foster carer is considering becoming a Shared Lives carer, they will need advice and support early to register with the local scheme, and information on how this will affect them financially, given that they are likely to receive a significant financial reduction. The introduction of Staying Put regulations outlined in the Care Act 2014 has allowed a more flexible approach to maintaining foster care arrangements. Staying Put is targeted at young people who have 'established familial relationships' with their foster carers, and offers this group the opportunity to remain with their carers until they reach the age of 21 (DfE 2010).

In cases where the young person lacks capacity, a decision needs to be made in their best interests as to whether they remain with the current foster carer. If there are no close family members who are able to assist in this decision-making, the young person should be referred to an IMCA to ensure that their views are represented, and that remaining with the foster carer is truly in their best interests.

TRANSITION PRACTITIONER TIPS

- Where a young person is leaving their foster carers, include in their support planning what, if any, contact will be maintained, and how this will be supported.

- Consider capacity at an early stage to ensure that a young person is appropriately supported through the transition process, and refer to an IMCA if necessary.

- Find out about Staying Put. If the young person has been placed in the foster placement by another authority, how long will that authority continue to fund this until alternative arrangements are made?

- Where a foster carer is keen to remain caring under a Shared Lives scheme, ensure that they have written information about the scheme and the opportunity to meet with workers from the team to discuss what is involved and to explore the financial implications.

CONCLUSION

This chapter has explained that young people may enter transition from a variety of backgrounds and routes, and this can have an impact on how transition practitioners may need to support them as they move from children's to adult services. Although most transition practitioners will take on case responsibility at age 18, there may be others who work under both children's and adults' legislation. Either way, the success of the transition is dependent, as always, on children's and adults services working together to establish the needs and wishes of that young person, and to develop a plan as they enter adulthood. Developing good working relationships with workers from the Children with Disabilities Teams is fundamental to achieving many of the suggestions identified in the 'Transition practitioner tips'.

RESOURCES

A Transition Guide for All Services can be found at the Transition Information Network website: *www.transitioninfonetwork.org.uk/resources/policy-guidance/a-transition-guide-for-all-services.aspx.*

For information around looked-after children, see The Who Cares? Trust website: *www.thewhocarestrust.org.uk.*

For information on residential schools, see the Special Needs UK website: *www.specialneedsuk.org.*

For information around autism and Asperger's, see The National Autistic Society website: *www.autism.org.uk.*

4

TRANSITIONS AND PERSONALISATION

INTRODUCTION

This chapter aims to provide an overview of the legislative background to the personalisation agenda, and its relevance to young people in transition. It provides good practice guidelines as to how practitioners working within the transition service user group can use personalisation to better promote the outcomes for the young people they are working with by working in partnership with key services, providing good information, and supporting the young people and their families effectively during their transition. It also provides an overview of self-directed support and its effectiveness for this group. It aims to evidence why specific transition workers, or a team of dedicated workers, working within a scope of young people aged at least 16+, are best placed to make personalisation work effectively within transition in order for the young people to achieve positive outcomes in their adult life. It also gives an overview of the Care Bill and its specific responsibilities for young people experiencing transition, with extended duties on the local authority to provide early assessment, continuity of support, and provision of the right information.

WHY IS PERSONALISATION IMPORTANT IN TRANSITION?

Social work practice within adult services has undergone significant policy changes since the Direct Payments Act in 1996. The personalisation of these services has been key to the changes, and the shared ambition across government is to put people first, through a radical reform of public services. Personalisation, including a strategic shift towards early invention and prevention, is regarded as the cornerstone of public services, with the intention being that everyone who receives services will have increased choice and control over how that is planned and delivered.

Personalisation is key to better outcomes for young people in transition. If it is implemented effectively at this stage, it can provide a blueprint for the young person's adult life, which gives them genuine choice and control over their housing options, employment, and how their care and support needs can be met. This provides transition workers with a framework as to how to arrange and provide these services. However, as transition starts for the young person at age 14, there can be no 'one size fits all' approach. Direct payments may be seen as the first stepping-stone to personalised services for young people with additional needs who are assessed as requiring care. The Community Care (Direct Payments) Act 1996 came into force in 1997, but direct payments were initially only available to a specific subsection of service users. This was later extended to include, among other groups, 16- and 17-year-olds, but also the parents and carers of children with disabilities. This Act is used in conjunction with the Children Act 1989, which is used to assess children who are defined as 'in need' by virtue of them having a disability, and is underpinned by the *Framework for the Assessment of Children in Need and their Families* (DH *et al.* 2000).

DIRECT PAYMENTS

Direct payments are intended to empower people to have choice and control over how their care is delivered; the method was to provide them with a cash equivalent to purchase their own services, in lieu of a local authority simply providing their care. However, for young people, direct payments only give a limited choice as to how their care is implemented. At ages 16 and 17, this can be limited to a choice as to who they wish to provide their care (this could be an agency or a Connexions worker personal advisor), and they have choice as to their schedule (when their care is delivered), but there are limits as to how the money is spent, and it is usually restricted to meeting personal care or social support needs. This does not meet the young person's needs holistically, and nor does it meet outcomes outside of this specific sphere of their life.

LEGISLATIVE AND POLICY BACKGROUND

Post-18 the differences can be significant in the provision of personalised and person-centred services, which are further-reaching than purely care and support. The overarching legislative statute for adults requiring community care is the NHS and Community Care Act 1990. This enabled the assessment and provision of services and support to help people to live as independently as possible. *Valuing People*, a government White Paper (DH 2001), laid out a series of developments that were required to be implemented to improve the lives, and life chances, of people with a learning disability in the UK. The first of these priorities was to better support young people in transition into adult life, and this was to be met by a Connexions worker Personal Adviser (PA) who would identify support needs and opportunities for the young person; in terms of adult social care, it suggested stronger links between children's and adult services. The White Paper also recognised the need for people with a learning disability to have increased choice and control over their services, and for this to be met with a direct payment where assessed as appropriate. Other key developments were to be supporting carers, good health, and housing, fulfilling lives, employment and advocating partnership working.

This can be seen as laying the groundwork for personalisation for adults with a learning disability. The government Green Paper, *Independence, Well-being and Choice* (DH 2005), and the White Paper, *Our Health, Our Care, Our Say* (DH 2006), also laid out proposals for the future direction of social care, based around four central tenets for transforming how social care was to be delivered. These were: better prevention and earlier intervention; more choice for individuals; tackling inequalities; and improved access to community-based services and more support for people with long-term needs.

In 2007 a government circular was published, *Putting People First* (HM Government 2007), to support the transformation of social care using the White Paper as an outline – it described the vision for a personalised approach to social care. This required councils to move to a system of individual budgets for everyone who had been assessed as eligible for social care services. It also gave councils a duty for the provision of information, advice and advocacy for all those requiring services and their carers, regardless of their eligibility for funded services.

Valuing People Now (DH 2009a) was a three-year government strategy building on the work of *Valuing People* by providing key messages and principles, but also what needed to happen to fully implement it. The four principles of this were: people with a learning disability have the same human rights as everyone else; they were to have greater choice and control over their support to enable them to manage everyday life, including greater access to housing employment, education, leisure and transport; they were to be involved and in control of decisions made about them, and have support and information to understand options and consequences to make informed choices; and they were to be enabled to participate in all aspects of the community, to be part of social networks and able to access goods and services. This promotes the principles of personalisation in terms of commissioning their own services and having control over the delivery of services. In order to implement this, the government recognised that they needed to develop leadership, delivery and structure. Local authorities needed to develop partnership boards that involved decision-makers in conjunction with authentic involvement from people with a learning disability and their carers. Commissioners within local authorities also needed to be supportive of the right outcomes, as well as the professionals working directly with service users, which required effective support and training in providing this. Local authorities and the NHS also had to measure how well they were implementing this strategy.

The central theme of personalisation is one of choice for the person accessing services. This begins with person-centred planning, which could provide the foundation for workers to support individuals in achieving these choices. This approach starts by 'treating people as individuals with a unique history and personality and listens to their voice' (Ahmed 2009). Research has found that individuals have more choice and control in determining their support and how it is delivered when personalisation is used with person-centred planning and personal budgets (Glendinning *et al.* 2008). *Valuing People Now* (DH 2009b) identified person-centred planning as a priority for young people in transition as a mechanism for allowing them to garner more choice and control over their future lives. This approach within the assessment process looks at people's capacity rather than their deficits, and seeks to address the support they need to achieve the outcomes they have identified.

TRANSITION WORKER ROLE

This combination of legislation and policy provides the framework under which practitioners implement personalisation for individuals. Transition workers must understand the duties and requirements this places on their practice, as well as an understanding of the *Framework for Assessment of Children in Need and their Families* (DH *et al.* 2000), in order to fully support and navigate young people and their families through this complex and cumbersome system, to achieve best outcomes. Part of the argument for a dedicated transition team must be that this enables the young people and their family's continuity, by having one worker to support them through this, and understand both the systems and the legislation in both children's and adult services. This is as opposed to a children's worker who hands over at age 18 to an adult worker who needs to get to know the young person, and understand them and their views as well as their needs, while providing them with services and support.

The process for transition for the young person starts at age 14, with the transition review at school. This is the young person and their family or carer's opportunity to discuss and explore the outcomes that they want to achieve following leaving school, whether this is further education, employment, meaningful day opportunities or moving on to independent living. There is a duty on the local authority to ensure that someone attends this review in order to advise and support, but also to record what is discussed and decided in order to inform future workers. Transition workers may have begun their involvement at this point, or they may start later in the young person's life, at age 16 or 17, depending on the make-up and structure of the team.

Transition workers may be involved before the young adult is 18, either alongside the children's worker or holding full case responsibility. In this case, they would be responsible for the statutory child in need reviews if the young person is in receipt of a service. Transition workers should use these reviews as opportunities to gather the information that will be relevant to their assessment and their adult life, alongside the process of reviewing their services. This should provide them with an opportunity to get to know the child, as well as the family or involved carers, and allow the child to build up a relationship of trust with them. These early reviews prior to the completion of the adult assessment can build on these relationships. They can also provide the opportunity to gather information from the school. Educational involvement can take many forms, such as the specific teacher or teaching assistant sharing what they know about the young person, likes and dislikes, as well as their preferred methods of communication, and what motivates and inspires the young person.

Transition workers can also undertake observations within the classroom in order to get a better understanding of the young person and how they interact within their peer group. This qualitative data, based on a deeper understanding of the young person, enables them to produce a more holistic and person-centred assessment. This combination of listening, observing and seeking information from other sources is good social work practice for all social workers, but particularly for those working in transition, as this can be used to fully understand the individual's choices and abilities. Working in this way also prevents an over-reliance on information from parents who may present a more one-dimensional view of their child, with an emphasis on risk and need rather than the child's strengths and abilities.

CASE STUDY – JULIE

Julie was 17 years old with a severe learning disability, and attending a special school. She had begun exhibiting some challenging behaviour and some anxiety. As part of her reviews the school expressed that they felt she had 'plateaued' within education, and were concerned about their ability to manage her on a long-term basis, despite her being eligible for a further 18 months in education. The practitioner worked with the school and Julie's family to explore adult provision options, and identified a local day care provision. Community support was ruled out due to her mother's need for a break from caring, and it was felt that Julie's behaviour could not be safely managed without a physical base. The provider was introduced to Julie, and the school funded her to attend two days a week, with social care funding support during the holidays. When Julie turned 18 she began attending full time, but by progressing her transition in a phased way, in partnership with all of the key people in Julie's life, this limited her distress and anxiety about the change.

Close links with local special schools and colleges can be invaluable to a transition team. They can provide a basis for mutual information-sharing – identification of children who may be eligible for a specialist transition service provides a good basis for financial forecasting for local authorities as well as a more timely service for the young person. Teachers are also able to identify who is struggling in the school environment, who is benefiting from educational input, and who would continue to benefit from further educational opportunities. A local special school can be a point at which transition workers can meet families and family carers, to provide information, guidance and support, and this can be done in a number of ways. Transition workers could facilitate drop-in sessions or appointment-based sessions for families to meet the dedicated worker and to find out what local options are available for the young person on leaving school. This could also give families the opportunity to ask about the assessment process, and what this might mean for them. Schools could also host events to provide a forum for further education provision and specialist adult providers for young people and their families to access, to enable them to request information and guidance, and to gather ideas about the kind of opportunities that are available. Transition workers can be key to these types of events, whether it is as part of the planning of the event, or attending the event to provide service information.

A young person with challenging behaviour combined with complex needs, for example, may not be best served by continued access to the traditional methods of education provision. A better outcome for that young person may be to start their transition early on to an adult provider that can provide education-based outcomes in the community or outdoor-based specialist provision. This can be achieved by transition workers working closely with the school to access education budgets to plan this with them and the young person and their family. This can serve as an early transition, in which the young person can become familiar with adult provision and staff teams, while building confidence for the family that their young person can progress outside of the traditional school environment.

For young people who would benefit from further educational opportunities, transition workers need to work closely with the school and SEN workers, to produce a learners with learning difficulties and/or disabilities (LLDD) assessment or a Section 139A assessment to identify appropriate local college provision or residential provision to meet that young person's educational outcomes (this will be replaced with an EHC plan; see Chapter 2 for more details). This may be via an appropriate life skills course or vocational opportunity, or an academic course of study. These assessments can be based within school reviews, which transition workers should attend, or an appointment at the young person's home. This can often be a source of conflict for SEN workers and transition workers, as they are the gatekeepers of two separate budgets. If a young person is not offered the education provision of their choice, this will often mean a larger budget is needed from the social care budget. (This is discussed further in Chapter 2.)

ONE-PAGE PROFILE

One of the tools used as part of person-centred planning for a young person is a one-page profile (see Appendix 2). Transition teams or individual workers can look at the use of one-page profiles and how they can be used to support young people, and their families and carers. This short document, completed by the young person and their family or carers, summarises the key points to support that young person well. Its purpose is that it provides a person-centred description and summary of information about that young person that people can use to either get to know them quickly, or ensure that the support that they are offering is consistent with the way the person wishes it to be delivered. The profiles are presented typically in three sections – what is important to the person, how they like to be supported, and what other people like and admire about the person – in a format that does not exceed one A4 sheet (see Appendix 2).

The uses of the one-page profile can be multiple – for example, for a young person who is moving from a special school where they have attended for many years, the staff that know them well could produce a one-page profile with the support of the teaching team and their family and peers. This could then travel with the young person to a local college or residential college, and the information could then be picked up readily by the new staff team in order to get the best out of the young person, as well as the young person feeling well supported and confident in the change.

Another good use of the one-page profile is when a young person is moving on from their home to supported living in the community. Although assessments are completed by the provider, and also by the practitioner, the one-page profile can present the key elements of this to the staff members, who can then get an instant sense of how the young person wants to be supported, and what they like to do. This is also equally applicable when a young person moves from children's respite provision to adult provision, or when their domiciliary care agency changes at 18. They are equally valuable to the practitioners who are assessing the young person if they have been completed at school or at home – they can be presented to them at their first visit to give them a very person-centred description of the person they are there to assess.

One-page profiles can prove vital to a young person who has specific needs around their communication methods. This could prevent the young person from telling someone their wishes, views or needs, but if a one-page profile is available, this will inform the person how best to communicate, what methods to use, and what works well for them. This reduces the risk of the young person being misunderstood or misinterpreted.

They can also then be stored for future workers to access when the responsibility transfers to other teams or workers. It should be noted, however, that this tool is not restricted to this service user group, but could be viewed as good practice to support whoever you may be working with – the value for an older person with dementia moving into residential care could be equally beneficial in terms of sharing key information quickly.

They can also have the unintentional benefit of supporting the family or carers to feel more involved in the transition, by giving them the opportunity to produce or participate in developing the profile. Transition has been described by parents or carers as a time when they feel powerless – involving them as fully as possible can empower them, but also helps them to focus their thinking on what is important to the young person in their future adult life, and what is important for other people to know about them. It is also a very strengths-based approach, which is important, as many of the assessments carried out with the young people and their families can be overly reliant on needs, and an emphasis on what the young person is unable to do – the one-page profile provides an important shift in how the young person and their family views the situation they are in.

The practitioner's role within this is to promote one-page profiles with parents but also in the education setting, as a positive step towards a good transition for the young person they support. Much of the information gathered from the profile can be incorporated within their adult assessment to ensure that the young person has a voice within that document.

ASSESSMENT PROCESS

The assessment is the first step to determining eligibility for a service, but also to identify support needs, to ascertain a budget, and to begin that young person's journey into personalised services.

Self-directed support is seen as the ideal vehicle to give the young person and their family as much control over how, when, and by whom their support is delivered. Leadbeater, Bartlett and Gallagher (2008) suggest that by using self-directed support the practitioner retains an overview of the quality and the outcomes, but becomes more like an adviser and broker, to support people to make good choices.

In Control (2011) developed a seven-step model to plot the process for self-directed support, following the local authority assessment of need and eligibility.

The first step they identified is *setting the budget* – if a young person is to plan their support, it is essential for them to know, up front, how much money can be used. Most local authorities use RAS to determine the budget that they are entitled to following the assessment.

The second step is *planning the support*. The support plan should lay out what the support will look like and what it will achieve as an outcome. For example, the young person could use a PA who will support them to access the community, and to access their health appointments and take them to the gym as part of the plan; the outcome of this would be that it improves and maintains their physical health and wellbeing, and also prevents social isolation. The support plan should also encompass the support networks that the young person already has in place – for example, if the young person has an older sibling who regularly takes them to the cinema and out to eat, this should be represented within the plan. Working in this way encourages the young person to examine the strengths they already have in their life, and may serve to formalise some of the more informal links they have to maximise their opportunities.

Agreeing the plan is the third step, where the practitioner signs off the plan on behalf of the local authority to ensure that the plan is safe and that risk-taking is considered and agreed, and confirms the budget.

Organising the money is viewed as the fourth step, which draws on issues of risk, responsibility and capacity, and this can be an area of contention for some families. Decisions need to be made and agreed as to who will manage the money, and who will be responsible for the ongoing management of the budget. This is sometimes clear-cut, with the young person having the ability and willingness to do this themselves. However, if they are unable or unwilling, it then needs to be established if they are able to nominate someone who is able, or if someone else needs to be found to do this on their behalf. The issues around capacity are addressed more fully in Chapter 8.

The fifth step is *organising the support*. How this is done is dependent on how the money has been organised, and what is specified in the support plan. This may involve the young person interviewing and recruiting a PA, but it may involve the practitioner supporting the young person to commission a service from an agency or a day service.

CASE STUDY – JOHN

John is a young man with a severe physical disability which has resulted in him being a wheelchair user. He received support from children's services to provide him with a PA. Within his transitional planning he identified that his current PA wasn't effective due to their time restrictions. By working with John a year prior to his eighteenth birthday, the practitioner was able to identify what his future budget would be, and help him to recruit new assistants to support him, both within further education, but also to access volunteering opportunities and social activities. He was able to identify that he wished his mother to manage his budget on his behalf. This reduced the 'cliff edge' of his eighteenth birthday, and helped him make effective plans to take him into adulthood in a way that he felt in control of.

Living life can be seen as the sixth step, and in many ways the most important for the young person, in terms of accessing the right support to live a good life, to experience and participate. The local authority retain a statutory duty to review the support plan, to measure the effectiveness in meeting outcomes, and this is the final step identified by In Control.

This review can be more frequent in the early stages of a support plan in order to ensure that things are working, and also to give the young person the opportunity to change what isn't working.

In Control have completed two national surveys of personal budgets to establish the impact that they have had on the lives of individuals and their families. The surveys found that over 70 per cent of people holding a budget reported a positive impact on being independent, getting the support that they want, and being supported with dignity. Over 60 per cent reported a positive impact on their physical health, mental wellbeing and control over their support. A further 50 per cent reported a positive impact on feeling safe in and outside their homes, and in relation to their paid carers. The survey found only small numbers of people reporting a negative impact.

Other key findings from the survey were that local authorities continue to find some aspects of the delivery process difficult. It appeared that there was a high level of positivity in respect of the impact, but far less positivity in the process of accessing a personal budget. It also reported less impact in specific areas of people's lives, including choosing where and who to live with, relationships with families and friends, gaining employment and volunteering. In terms of young adults in transition, these are the areas that young people require high levels of support with, and that have been identified as being key outcome areas for young people. How to work positively within these areas is looked at in greater depth in further chapters, but it is apparent that practitioners need to find positive methods of working with, and engaging young people to work towards, these outcomes in a more effective way.

It can therefore be seen that initial legislation introduces the concept of personalisation, but then reinforces the key elements of this in successive legislation. It is also clear that support for the service user that is self-directed as opposed to being arranged by the practitioner and arranged by the local authority is seen as the ideal vehicle for personalisation. However, the service users were disappointed by the implementation and bureaucratic process needed to access a personal budget. The Care Act 2014 aims to standardise the process for implementing personalisation further, and it provides a legal duty for local authorities to assess, provide a care and support plan, and provision of a personal budget. It has eleven key elements of reform for care and support, summarised here:

- *Improving information*: local authorities now have a responsibility to provide comprehensive information with regard to the services and providers in their area, so the public can access services that provide early intervention, make informed choices, are able to choose from a wide range and are able to access independent financial advice.

- *Entitlement to public care and support*: it provides a consistent approach to establish eligibility for care and support, introducing the same rights for carers. It also gives individuals the right to ask the local authority to arrange their care regardless of who is funding the package.

- *National framework for eligibility*: it introduces a national framework to ensure a consistent minimum eligibility criteria throughout England. This will replace the current system of FACS (SCIE 2013). It will also give local authorities a duty to assess anyone who appears in need of support, regardless of financial circumstances.

- *Personalisation*: this gives the local authority a legal responsibility to provide a care and support plan, a personal budget, and the full costs of a plan to meet their requirements regardless of how this is funded, and then responsibility to review and monitor that support plan.

- *Financial assessment*: this sets out a clear approach to charging, to help people understand how much they will have to contribute. The new regulations will ensure that everyone will have their finances assessed in the same way, which takes into account their income and assets.

- *Capping care costs*: this will allow the establishment of a cap on care costs, currently estimated to be £72,000 from April 2016.

- *Deferred payment agreements*: there will be a legal right for people to defer paying care home costs, meaning they do not have to sell their home in their lifetime.

- *Safeguarding*: this provides a clear framework to protect vulnerable adults at risk of abuse or neglect. Although local authorities have taken primary responsibility for safeguarding, this has lacked a clear set of laws or regulations to underpin it, leaving the responsibility and accountability between agencies unclear.

▫ *Carers*: the Act gives carers the same rights as the people they care for.

▫ *Moving area*: this provides clear guidelines for continuity of care, for people wishing to move between local authority areas.

▫ *Provider failure*: local authorities will have a clear responsibility to ensure both residential care and care provided in a person's home; if a care provider fails, this will be regardless of how that care is funded.

▫ *Transition from child to adult*: this will give young people and their carers a right to request an assessment prior to the child turning 18.

(Cohen 2013)

THE CARE ACT 2014 AND TRANSITION

The Care Act 2014 gives local authorities specific duties with regard to young people in transition from childhood to adult care and support services. The Act says that if a child or carer of a child is likely to have eligible needs when they become 18, they must be assessed, regardless of whether they are currently in receipt of services. It also places a duty on the practitioner assessing to provide advice and information about meeting or reducing their needs, as well as giving the young person and their carer an indication of the support they can expect. It is hoped that this will remove some of the uncertainty at having to wait until the age of 18. This can be met within the provision of a dedicated transition team or worker by using a tracker system that can plot the eligible young people, by working in partnership with children's services, and also the special schools within the local area.

The Act also states that the person does not have to be a certain age in order to request an assessment, removing any blanket rule about age, and instead giving the local authority the flexibility to work around the person involved, recognising that the best time to plan is often different for each person. It also requires that if a young person is accessing services via children's services, this must be continued through the assessment process, ensuring that there is no 'cliff edge' to services for the person. Again, by working in partnership with children's teams, providing services to children with disabilities can ensure early intervention and early co-working, with effective handovers and information transfer.

The Act is intended to dovetail with the Children and Families Bill, in the creation of their birth to 25 years EHC plan for all children and young adults with additional needs. Where the person is 18, the care element will potentially be met by provisions under the Care Act. It also aims to improve cooperation between all of the services that are involved in the support of young people, to ensure that the necessary people work together, that the correct information, advice and support are available, and that assessments can be carried out jointly where necessary (DH 2013a).

There are also several areas of overlap between the Children and Families Act and the Care Act that potentially strengthen practitioners' approach to delivering a personalised service for young people in transition.

Both the Children and Families Act 2014 and the Care Act 2014 have a focus on outcomes. The Children and Families Act is explicit about the outcomes that require focus from Year 9: employment, health, living independently and friends and relationships. This is echoed in the Care Act for post 18 but also includes the suitability of their accommodation, economic wellbeing and a duty to provide services. They both provide the local authority with a duty to promote the young person's wellbeing, which is the central tenet of the Care Act.

The Children and Families Act provides a framework for a single coordinated process for assessment, with an EHC plan for young people with SEN which can continue to the age of 25. The assessment should be person-centred, with a focus on preparing for adulthood. Both Acts have given an emphasis to carers with both pieces of legislation providing a duty to local authorities to assess parents, carers and also young carers. The Care Act also echoes the duty to assess children and young people, with a proviso that this can be requested at any time by the young person or their family, but also that there is a duty to assess when there is a likelihood that there will be care and support needs post 18. Both Acts emphasise the need for involvement and participation from the young person, to make the process person-centred with a focus on their identified outcomes.

There are also significant overlaps in the commissioning strategies that will underpin the frameworks of the two pieces of legislation. They both promote integration of health and care provision to promote the wellbeing of the young person; the Children and Families Act includes education as part of this, recognising the importance of combining the strands of provision for the young person. Both Acts also give provision for the use of Direct Payments, with the Children and Families Act giving the young person a right to request this, but the Care Act strengthening this by stating 'must include a personal budget'. Both pieces of legislation also include the requirement for partners to cooperate, to better meet the needs of young people. The Care Act takes the commissioning slightly further with the inclusions of improving the quality of the care and support offered and the need to better develop the market in order to provide real choices for adults spending their budgets with confidence in the services that are offered. This is perhaps in response to recent scandals following documentaries into the care provided within adult service providers.

CONCLUSION

In conclusion, this chapter has demonstrated how a dedicated transition worker, or team, working within a larger age range than the traditional 18+ group, is best placed to work within the personalisation agenda to ensure the best outcomes for young people to live a fulfilling adult life. It has provided the legislative overview of the personalisation movement, and has given examples of best practice for transition workers to apply this to their practice. It has also provided links to the Care Act 2014, as it currently stands, and evidenced how transition workers can meet the additional requirements.

5

TRANSITIONS AND EMPLOYMENT

INTRODUCTION

A typical question asked of secondary school children would be, 'What do you want to be when you grow up?'. This question, however, appears to be avoided when talking to young people of the same age in the special school system. This could be because people feel that young people with a learning disability or additional needs may be unwilling or unable to access employment opportunities, or because of an expectation that their adult life will somehow be different from others of the same age.

The way society views people with a learning disability has changed dramatically over time. The Victorian era saw the creation of asylums that aimed to educate and develop the skills of people with learning disabilities, but as they had underestimated the numbers of these individuals, they quickly became overcrowded and moved to workhouses. At this point, medical professionals shifted the focus to one of diagnosis, away from the original aims of education and social care (Carnaby 2002).

The Industrial Revolution shifted this further, as the focus was on societal productivity, and people with a learning disability, at that time, were seen as unable to contribute. This saw the advent of institutional care as a means of segregating people who were viewed as unable to contribute outside of their own communities (Carnaby 2002). However, within these institutions value was placed on employment and working roles. Patients were allocated work roles depending on their 'grades', which was a hierarchical measure of how 'able' the person was. Male jobs included manual labour, and female jobs included laundry and domestic work, but also caring for the less able. The higher-grade jobs would give the patient a higher rate of pocket money and a greater degree of independence, but also a higher status. These job roles provided the institutions with a method of exercising control of the patients by providing strict routines and timetables, and also segregation of the sexes (Atkinson, Jackson and Walmsley 1997).

It wasn't until the 1971 White Paper, *Better Services for the Mentally Handicapped* (DHSS 1971), that the concept of institutions was challenged, and the idea of moving people from institutions back into the community was established. However, it was not until the NHS and Community Care Act 1990 that a clear pathway for this to be achieved was provided, and a move back to the community was implemented (Carnaby 2002).

There is also now a clear drive for people with a learning disability to be supported into employment. An objective in the White Paper *Valuing People* is:

> To enable more people with learning disabilities to participate in all forms of employment, wherever possible in paid work, and to make a valued contribution to the world of work. (DH 2001, p.84)

The government's drive for equality for people with disabilities and learning disabilities in employment has also been reinforced via legislation and regulation. The Disability Discrimination Act (2005) has been updated so that it gives people with disabilities a fair chance at being considered for a job. It also ensures that reasonable adjustments are made for people with disabilities in the workplace, in order for them to be able to complete their work to the optimum standard.

The Equality Act 2010 offers protection to employees with a disability from discrimination, harassment and victimisation, as it defines disability as a 'protected characteristic'. This is applicable throughout the employment cycle, from recruitment, selection, employment terms and access to benefits and facilities right through to dismissal. It places a duty on employers to make 'reasonable adjustments' to enable the worker, or potential employee, to not be disadvantaged. This can mean adjustments to the working environment, the provision of aids or accessible information, provision of equipment or altering hours of work or training. This can be seen as powerful legislation to protecting the place of a person with disabilities within employment, as it makes failure to make a 'reasonable adjustment' illegal (Parker, Honigmann and Clements 2013).

The Care Act 2014 raises participation in employment explicitly within its definition of 'wellbeing', as well as the 'individual's contribution to society', and the local authority must have regard to these principles of wellbeing when implementing the Act.

There is a broad consensus regarding the benefits of employment, across multiple disciplines, disability groups, employers and all political parties, based on extensive clinical experience and on principles of fairness and social justice. When their health condition permits, people with disabilities should be encouraged and supported to be in work as soon as possible, because it is both therapeutic and also promotes recovery and rehabilitation. In addition to this it also promotes full participation in society, independence and human rights, and it reduces poverty and improves quality of life and wellbeing. People with disabilities who move off benefits and enter work generally experience improvements in income, socioeconomic status, mental and general health and wellbeing (Waddell *et al.* 2006).

There is a strong evidence base showing that work is generally good for physical and mental health and wellbeing, while worklessness is associated with poorer physical and mental health and wellbeing. Work can be therapeutic and can reverse the adverse health effects of unemployment. This is true for healthy people of working age, but also for many people with disabilities (Waddell *et al.* 2006).

There has been a widespread view that employment is impossible or inappropriate for young people with disabilities, particularly those with a learning disability, and that accessing social groups, day centres, pottery (for example) and outings are a viable alternative to accessing work. This is a dated misconception. Apart from it being economically rewarding, both for the individual and for society as a whole as a concept employment is a highly valued social activity. It alters a perception of an individual from a service user to that of a contributor, that they have skills, they are able to learn, they have a place in society and are contributing to the community in which they live and work (Williams 2006).

Despite the evidence that employment is good for the health, wealth and emotional wellbeing of a person with a disability, and the legislation that protects the rights of an individual with a disability in employment, less than 10 per cent of people with a learning disability are in employment; however around two-thirds of people with learning disabilities want to work (Carnaby 2002).

Current government policy has recognised that these employment outcomes are poor for children and young people with additional needs, and that the systems in place for supporting them into employment are complicated, difficult to access and expensive. To address this they recognise that young adults with disabilities and additional needs, including those with more complex needs, should be supported to develop skills and gain qualifications and experience to succeed in their chosen career paths. To achieve these aims they have outlined this vision in *Fulfilling Potential: Making it Happen for Disabled People* (ODI and DWP 2013), in conjunction with the reforms to SEN and the disability system in the new Children and Families Act 2014.

The economic rationale that underpins this strengthens the need for reform further. A report by the National Audit Office (NAO 2011) estimated that supporting one person with a learning disability into employment could increase that person's income between 55–95 per cent, and equipping them with the skills to live semi-independently, rather than in a supported setting, could reduce lifetime support costs to the public of £1 million. This is in addition to improving that person's quality of life, independence and self-esteem, and the wider benefits for employers, families, the local community and wider society (NAO 2011).

GOVERNMENT INITIATIVE TO SUPPORT EMPLOYMENT: DISABILITY CONFIDENT CAMPAIGN

In order to further support the employment agenda for people with disabilities, the government launched a two-year advertising campaign to support businesses to become more confident in recruiting and supporting people with disabilities in the workplace. This is intended to tackle employers' attitudes towards workers with disabilities following research where jobseekers cited this as a bigger barrier to employment (42%) than transport difficulties (37%).

In order to support businesses, the government has pledged to:

- host regional business breakfasts on proposals for a dedicated employer service

- roll out a campaign to target employers' and workforce attitudes to hiring disabled people

- support business-led commitments to recruit more disabled people

- support media organisations to increase the representation and portrayal of disabled people in the media

- provide opportunities via access to work to engage disabled people in work experience, traineeships and supported internships

- provide advice and support to employers on hiring and keeping disabled people in work.

(DWP 2014)

BARRIERS TO DISABLED YOUNG PEOPLE IN TRANSITION GAINING EMPLOYMENT

There are a number of barriers that make it difficult for people with a learning disability to access employment:

- *Lack of appropriate training*: many people with a learning disability do not have access to quality further education and training. Only one in three adults with a learning disability takes part in any education or training.

- *Lack of appropriate support*: people with a learning disability often need support to develop key skills for work and to find and get a job. They may need support in the workplace. Government disability employment programmes do not always meet the needs of people with a learning disability.

- *The welfare system*: there are certain structural barriers within the benefits system that can make it very difficult for people with a learning disability to achieve their aspiration to work. For example, the amount of money that can be earned by recipients of welfare benefits without their benefits being affected is extremely low.

This can mean that people are not necessarily any better off if they work. The consequence is that people with a learning disability can remain trapped in poverty, reliant on welfare benefits, and unable to contribute to society.

- *Employers' attitudes*: many employers are reluctant to take on someone with a learning disability. This might be because they do not know enough about the benefits of employing people with a learning disability, or they do not know how to get the right support. Stigma and discrimination about people with a learning disability are still widespread. For young people with a physical disability, the employer would have to contribute to any adaptations that would need to be made. This can be off-putting to a potential employer.

- *Family*: family carers can often feel that employment can be risky for their young person, often for many of the reasons listed above. The step from the protected environment of a school to the world of employment is a huge shift, which can leave family carers feeling fearful.

- *Professionals' attitudes*: the professionals involved with the young person can often be risk-averse, and may subconsciously (or consciously) steer the young person's thinking away from employment because it can be a risky transition, which, if attempted at the wrong point, can impact on the young person's confidence. If a first attempt at employment is a negative one, it can be difficult to provide or access the intensive support needed for the young person to adjust to the change or to the new pathways offered.

- *Special school system*: for young people within the special school system, there is often little or no emphasis on paid employment as a viable option on leaving school. Schools can often have a paternalistic attitude towards their pupils, which can result in a risk-averse culture where they are steered towards further education or day opportunities as a stepping-stone out of the school environment rather than a shift to support them looking for paid employment.

(Mencap 2014)

ROUTES INTO EMPLOYMENT

The routes into employment for a young person with a disability are often the same that any young person has available to choose from. However, they need to be carefully considered in terms of the additional support needed, with additional thinking around contingency planning and risk enablement for the young person.

FURTHER AND HIGHER EDUCATION

LOCAL COLLEGE

Most young people leaving specialist schools will have been given the opportunity via the school curriculum to attend the further education colleges that are located within their home community. These are often mainstream further education colleges offering specialist courses designed for people with a learning disability that will build on their core skills in English and Maths, as well as incorporating life skills or further developing existing interests that the young person may have.

SPECIALIST RESIDENTIAL COLLEGE

There are over 70 specialist residential colleges across England, Wales and Ireland. These may be located within cities or more rurally.

College courses traditionally include art and crafts, media and IT, horticulture, administration, horse-based learning, or retail and hospitality. They should provide a focus on learning skills that will help the young person develop into adult life, including managing their own money, shopping, budgeting and travel training. They provide the opportunity for young people to live within their peer group, and extend their range of experience towards new activities and learning new skills as well as providing opportunities to engage in voluntary work or work experience.

Specialist colleges are different from schools as they offer a broader range of courses and work experience, with the chance to take part in voluntary work. The professional facilities at college are of the same high standards that you would find in the workplace, and colleges have good links with local businesses and the community, which gives students the chance to take part in valuable work experience.

The decision as to whether a young person is offered a place at a residential or local college can be a complex one, and is subject to a LLDD assessment, which is commissioned by the Local Education Authority. The rule of thumb for these decisions (explored more fully in Chapter 2), are generally made on the basis of whether the young person's educational needs can be met in their local area – if they can be met via a local college course, that is what is offered. For young people for whom their educational needs cannot be met at a local college, the search may be widened to a specialist residential college.

TRANSITION PRACTITIONER TIPS

- Ensure that families and young people are aware of the options on offer.

- Ensure that a LLDD assessment is accessed at the earliest stage possible to allow time for any decisions to be challenged, particularly if residential college is the young person's preferred option.

- Ensure that the options are in line with the young person's wishes and interests and use any skills previously learned.

UNIVERSITY EDUCATION

For young adults whose disability is a physical limitation, they may wish to consider higher education at university as a route into potential employment as graduates. There are additional monies available to support students who choose this option. The Disabled Students' Allowance (DSA) is a supplementary benefit allowance that is available to students,who have additional expenses as a direct result of their disability. This is not a means-tested allowance, but is subject to an assessment, and must be evidenced by health professionals before they are able to apply.

There are four elements of DSA support:

- *Non-medical help*: for students requiring non-medical personal assistance, for example, readers for blind students or note-takers or scribes for students who are unable to make their own notes.

- *Specialist equipment allowance*: for help with the purchase of equipment necessary because of the student's disability, for example, computer, Braille printer, Dictaphone, specialist software, and so on.

- *General allowance*: for general expenses arising from attendance at the course, for example, extra photocopying, special dietary requirements, and so on.

- *Travel allowance*: extra travel costs that have to be paid as a result of disability, and not normally for everyday travel costs.

If a student has personal care needs, whether these are occasionally for showers, for example, or more intense needs that require a PA or 24-hour support provided by an agency, this remains the responsibility of the local authority to which they belong. A social worker or care manager would assess these needs, and funding would be provided to meet assessed needs.

If a student requires adaptations or equipment within the residential element of the university – the halls of residence, for example – these need to be addressed by an occupational therapist within the local authority in which the university is located, to ensure the student has a living environment that meets their physical needs.

TRANSITION PRACTITIONER TIPS

- When an institution has been chosen, make contact with the young person's disability adviser (with the young person's consent) to look at the practical issues early on, such as accommodation, travel between campus, accommodation, the canteen, etc. This will then help overcome any potential barriers early on.

- Ensure that a DSA assessment has been requested by the young person or their family in good time.

- Ensure that assessment for a personal budget is completed and a budget agreed to provide maximum opportunity for support planning, as there are many variables inherent in a move to a university, including staff recruitment (potentially from outside of the local area), allocation of accommodation, provision of a lecture timetable, and so on.

- If there are adjustments or equipment needed for the accommodation, a referral is needed for the occupational therapist – this can be made by the social worker, the young person or the university, but ensure that in discussions, the responsibility for this task is allocated and completed to ensure it does not hold up a move.

- Think about contingencies – if they do not get the grades for their preferred choice of university, what happens then?

- Housing Benefit can be applied for if the young person is in receipt of higher-rate DLA. However, this will not cover the cost of an additional sleep-in room if that is needed.

OTHER ROUTES INTO PAID EMPLOYMENT
SUPPORTED INTERNSHIPS

From August 2013 all young people in education where the student has additional needs evidenced by an LLDD assessment or EHC plan have been expected to follow a personalised learning programme. A supported internship is a learning programme aimed at young people who wish to move into paid employment, but who require extra support to do so. They are intended to enable young people to gain sustainable paid employment by equipping them with skills for work, via learning opportunities in the workplace. They normally last for a year, and include unpaid work placements of at least six months. They include a personalised study programme for relevant qualifications, including English and Maths, to the level appropriate for the learner. They offer a higher level of support to young people than a traditional apprenticeship or trainee programme, and also include a job coach within the workplace, and additional support for their non-workplace learning (DWP 2013a).

For the young person, the internship should contribute to their long-term career goals and fit within their capabilities. For the employer, it should meet a real business need, and the potential of a paid job at the end of the programme if the intern meets the standard required. The job coach should provide support to the employer as well as the young person. For the young person, the job coach provides in-work support, which should be reduced when the young person becomes comfortable and familiar with the tasks and expectations of the role. For the employer, the job coach should increase their confidence in offering and working with interns, and increasing their business case for a more diverse workforce.

Supported internships should reflect these conditions:

- The majority of the young person's time should be within the workplace.

- The young person should comply with the conditions of the workforce in terms of timekeeping and uniform or dress code.

- The correct approach for the young person to learn tasks should be used.

- Learning goals should be tailored to the young person's capabilities.

- There should be support from a job coach and tutor.

- Continued support should follow the programme.

(DWP 2013a)

TRANSITION PRACTITIONER TIPS

- Ensure regular reviews with the employer, job coach and the young person, as this will flag up any potential problems, and allow time for resolving these before they become a barrier. This will also allow targets to be set, and prevent drift.

- Regular communication with the young person ensures that it is meeting their needs and expectations, without the pressure of divulging issues in front of their employer.

ACCESS TO WORK FUND

From September 2013 young people starting work experience, work placements or traineeships who have a health condition or a disability could apply to the Department for Work and Pensions (DWP) for funding to support their access to these opportunities. They can apply for funding for:

- travel costs to get them to work

- the costs of any support workers or job coaches

- any specialist equipment that is necessary for them to complete their work tasks.

There is no set amount for an Access to Work grant, or for how much a person may receive (DWP 2013b).

The amount of approved support provided by Access to Work is dependent on whether the person is employed or self-employed, how long they have been in the job, and the type of support needed. The employee's needs will be assessed by an assessor who may visit them in their workplace. It is then the responsibility of the employer to arrange specialist support or equipment, which will be recouped by Access to Work. The employer continues to have a duty to the employee under the Equality Act 2010, even if they are eligible for Access to Work funding, and may still be required to make reasonable adjustments that are not funded via the scheme (Parker *et al.* 2013).

TRANSITION PRACTITIONER TIPS

- Provide support with the application process, or signpost to the correct source of support. This can feel overwhelming to a young person who is attempting to find employment.

- Ensure that the employer is aware of their responsibilities in supporting the young person.

WORK CHOICE

The Work Choice programme was launched in October 2010, and replaces the previous disability employment programmes, WORKSTEP and Work Preparation, and the Job Introduction Scheme, provided by the DWP.

Work Choice can support young people with disabilities to help them get and keep a job. The type of support that can be accessed depends on the help that is needed. This is obviously different for everyone, but can include:

- training and developing skills

- building confidence

- interview coaching

- finding a job that is appropriate, suitable and sustainable.

The level of support is determined via an interview with the DWP when Work Choice is applied for.

Work Choice is delivered by different providers across the country. They offer three levels of help, as outlined below:

Work entry support	
Advice on work and personal skills to help in finding a job	Up to six months
In-work support	
Help to start work and to stay in a job	Up to two years
Longer-term in-work support	
Help to get on in a job and work without support	Long-term

Work entry support can be extended by three or six months in exceptional circumstances, and when there is a clear prospect of a job.

To qualify for Work Choice an applicant must:

- be of working age

- need support in work as well as to find a job

- be able to work at least 16 hours a week after work entry support

- have a recognised disability that means they find it hard to get or keep a job

- need specialist help that they can't get from other government programmes or schemes – for example, workplace adjustments, or Access to Work.

People with disabilities can apply if they have a job but are at risk of losing the job because of their disability. This also applies if they are self-employed.

There are concerns that Work Choice, due to the way in which it has been commissioned as a performance-based funding regime, will concentrate its efforts on the most able young people as opposed to those with more complex needs (Samuel 2010). The eligibility criteria also suggest that the need to be able to work for more than 16 hours a week means that this is less achievable for some of the more complexly disabled young people experiencing their transition. The nature of some disabilities means that this would be a far less favourable option for some.

PROFESSIONAL DILEMMA

- The budget that is often awarded to those young people with complex physical needs is high, to take into account the personal care needs of that young person. If a young person has high personal care needs that need to be met, there is often little to spare for employment support. The dilemma is how this can be successfully balanced to ensure they receive the support they need alongside the support they want.

Many local authorities tender this responsibility out to private or voluntary associations. Mencap's Employ Me is one way that this can be commissioned (Mencap n.d.). It is a specialist programme to help people with a learning disability to gain paid employment, and can provide support in a number of ways:

- *Pre-employment support*: appropriate training to develop the skills needed to get a paid job

- *Work trials and placements*: experience in a real work environment

- *Support to find paid work*: help with searching for a paid job through a range of employers, CV writing and interview preparation

- *Job coaching and in-work support*: help to learn new skills and to cope with change.

Support can be offered to meet the needs and aspirations of each individual, and should be provided in a person-centred way, including support with evening and weekend work. It can be accessed in a number of ways using a personal budget or another form of direct payment, by paying with private funds, or with funding directly from a local authority or the DWP. A personal budget can only be accessed following an assessment from a social worker or care manager, with an identified need for support gaining work as an outcome of that assessment.

PROFESSIONAL DILEMMA

- For young people for whom paid work is an achievable outcome, their needs can often not generate a personal budget, or if it is generated, this can be quite minimal. Often the cost of employment services (when they are not contracted by the local authority, for example) can far outweigh the budget indicated. How can this professional dilemma be resolved to best support the young person into paid employment?

TRANSITION PRACTITIONER TIPS

- Identify if the service can be locally contracted, or if the young person needs a personal budget to buy the service needed.

- Review the support regularly to ensure it is meeting the needs of the young person, to ensure targets are being met and to prevent drift.

SOCIAL ENTERPRISES

Social enterprises are part of the growing 'social economy'. The social economy, sometimes referred to as the 'third sector', positions itself between the traditional private sector on the one hand, and the public sector on the other. It includes voluntary and community organisations, foundations and associations of many types.

Social enterprises are businesses that combine the entrepreneurial skills of the private sector with a strong social mission that is characteristic of the social economy as a whole. (New Horizons Partnership 2007)

A social enterprise will also have a clear sense of its 'social mission', which means it will know what difference it is trying to make, who it aims to help, and how it is going to go about it. Social enterprises make their money from selling goods and services, and should cover their own costs in the long term (although, like any business, they may need help to get started). They put at least half of any profits back into making a difference, and pay reasonable salaries to their staff (Social Enterprise UK 2014).

Social enterprises can provide powerful opportunities for people with learning disabilities to work within sectors or specific projects that interest them, and can also provide learning opportunities and skills development.

The standard and variety of social enterprises can vary locally, and it is difficult to know what is available as there is no standard listing for what is available by area. Some can also be very small-scale projects, which are more likely to be advertised by word of mouth than via formal routes.

TRANSITION PRACTITIONER TIPS

- Find out what social enterprises exist in the local area. Is there a dedicated person or service that provides a list of them?

- Are they able to meet the physical needs of the young person, or will they require a support worker to accompany the young person?

- How will the young person be paid for their work?

- Will it enable the young person to develop existing skills? Is it an area that they are interested in? If it isn't, will this be a sustainable option for the young person?

- Is the young person able to get there? Do travel arrangements need to be made?

VOLUNTEERING

People choose to volunteer for a variety of reasons. For some, it offers the chance to give something back to the community or to make a difference to the people around them. For others, it provides an opportunity to develop new skills or to build on existing experience and knowledge. Regardless of the motivation, what unites all volunteers is that they find it both challenging and rewarding.

Below are some of the reasons people choose to volunteer. For some it provides an opportunity to:

- give something back to an organisation that has impacted on a person's life, either directly or indirectly

- make a difference to the lives of others

- help the environment

- help others less fortunate or without a voice

- feel valued and part of a team

- gain confidence and self-esteem.

For others, volunteering can be a route to employment, or a chance to try something new that may lead to a career change. From this perspective, volunteering can be a way of:

- gaining new skills, knowledge and experience

- developing existing skills and knowledge

- enhancing a CV

- improving employment prospects

- gaining an accreditation

- using one's professional skills and knowledge to benefit others.

Volunteering may also appeal because of its social benefits. These include:

- meeting new people and making new friends

- a chance to socialise

- getting to know the local community.

There is also much anecdotal evidence that volunteering has a positive impact on health.

For young people with a learning or physical disability, volunteering can be seen as a positive route into employment. This can be incorporated into a schedule as it does not demand fixed hours, and it can be completed alongside education on a weekend or evening. It may often be seen by families or others supporting the young person as a taster of how they will manage a paid work environment, without the commitment or expectations that paid work can bring. It also has the ability to widen that young person's support networks, to involve other volunteers, paid workers and users of that specific service or environment.

TRANSITION PRACTITIONER TIPS

- Clarify what hours are being offered and the employer's expectation of the young person.

- Is there sufficient support for the young person there, or will additional support be required?

- Is there a possibility of this leading to paid employment?

CASE STUDY – NORTHAMPTONSHIRE PILOT

Northamptonshire commissioned a Community Connecting Pilot that aimed to provide focused support to their young people in transition, by working alongside them to identify their talents and interests, and to assist them in finding suitable community-based activities. Community connectors worked alongside their paid workers and families for a 12-week period to identify new ways of working within their local communities, including work opportunities, travel training, sports and gym activities, social groups and leisure activities. This intensive support provided a positive impact on the personal outcomes of the young people, who reported increased self-confidence, greater independence, increased involvement in social activities and use of public transport, and appropriate employment, both paid and voluntary.

It also had financial benefits, with reductions made to the cost of their ongoing services, with some needing reduced paid support, and in some cases, no paid support at all.

COMMISSIONING EMPLOYMENT SUPPORT

As supporting people with a disability into paid work is a policy priority for local authorities, it is up to the commissioners for the local authorities to determine which services to invest in to ensure that the local authority is receiving the best value for money, and also that the services are providing people with the best employment support to gain paid work.

Services nationally were reviewed in 2011 by NDTi to establish the economic evidence that underpins the different models of employment support. They found that the system of employment support was 'characterised by a complex, interrelated array of approaches, pilots and schemes which frame the issues in a variety of ways'. The key messages that came from the review were that there was evidence to support 'supported employment' as an effective solution to support people into paid jobs. However, it also found that there was little information published on the cost-effectiveness of differing schemes, and that the interpretation of supported employment differed significantly between services, which made it difficult to compare. They also found inconsistencies in the evidence relating to real savings to the taxpayer – for example, if someone was to work part-time and remain on benefits. They also found that research into newer approaches of supported employment was not well evidenced as they do not appear to have been used at national level or sustained. NDTi recommended further research to examine some of these gaps and inconsistencies (NDTi 2011).

Further research was then completed by NDTi to examine the relationship between investment and outcomes for employment support. This found that investment in spend from local authorities was levelling off and declining following a period of growth. It also found that only a third of the local authority spend was being used for the evidence-based models of employment support, as commissioners and services have little data to inform them how best to target their spend to ensure value for money. They found that the cost per job outcome ranged hugely, from £208 to £57,640, and averaged at £8217 per individual, and that the proportion of people securing paid employment was 38 per cent (NDTi 2013).

There was also limited evidence that personal budgets were being used to support people to gain or retain employment. The survey of employment providers found that only a third of those questioned had received any income via personal budgets in the previous 18 months, and the average number of people in the service using a personal budget was just three. They identified four factors that prevent or discourage the use of personal budgets for employment support:

- low demand from individuals or families

- professional attitudes towards employment support

- the personal budget process

- availability of good, evidence-based employment support.

From this they made four recommendations in response to these barriers:

- improved information and advice to increase individuals' knowledge and aspirations towards gaining employment by the use of their personal budget

- social workers recognising and giving priority to paid employment as an important social work outcome

- social work assessments considering employment as an outcome to enable the identification of funding via the personal budget process

- commissioners developing the market within their local area to ensure that there are good employment services for people to buy.

TRANSITION PRACTITIONER TIPS

- Become familiar with supported employment services within the local area. Visit and talk to the providers – establish what model is being used. This would allow you to discuss employment support with confidence with families and young people.

- Ensure that employment is discussed and encouraged as an outcome within the assessment process.

CONCLUSION

As can be seen from the sections above, there is huge variation in both the routes into employment and the support that may be needed to gain and sustain paid employment.

Transition workers need to knowledgeable, confident and realistic when discussing employment options. This ideally needs to begin very early on in the transition process, within school reviews. This is the first stage in workers getting to know, and understanding, the viewpoint of the young person, and finding out what they are good at and also what they are interested in, which should be integral to the school reviews. However, they can often be dominated by the educational aspects of the young person's life and measuring their progress against educational targets.

The school should be ideally placed to identify the young person's strengths and interests, and should support the young person and their family to think more widely about their future options. The school will often arrange work experience and volunteering opportunities as part of their wider curriculum. A good contact for transition workers is the person at the school responsible for arranging and sourcing these placements. If a young person is currently undertaking work experience at a nursing home, for example, and they are enjoying this and have identified they would like to work in this setting following school, then, by using the school's contacts, this can be further explored to see if they can offer paid work, or further experience that will support future paid work.

Events at the school that showcase services for young people beyond school should heavily feature employment services within the local area. This is beneficial for both the services and the young people and their families. It is powerful if people with disabilities who have used the service are part of the showcasing, as this gives a positive message for the young people considering employment. This can help families who are reluctant to consider employment to widen their thinking, and also shift the culture of thinking at the school. To hear from an individual who has gone through the process and achieved the outcome of paid work can alleviate a risk-averse attitude and encourage people to think more positively about employment as a viable outcome. For employment services this can also increase their prospects of attracting a cohort of new users that aren't yet restricted by a culture of day services and welfare dependency, that are enthusiastic and motivated about entering employment.

A key point in a young person's transition into adulthood and employment is that of leaving school. Therefore it is vital for transition workers to have started the assessment process, and to know the young person well prior to this point. As can be seen by the multitude of routes into employment, there is no single pathway that a young person can follow; rather, there is more of a labyrinth that requires careful navigation with support from the relevant circle of support around the young person. Paid employment for a young person with additional needs should be viewed as a win-win scenario for all involved in that young person's life. For the young person it provides improved life outcomes, including better mental and emotional health, a larger social network, reduced financial dependency and an improved community presence. For transition workers and the wider local authority it provides a person-centred, bespoke outcome for the person they are working with, with a reduced spend and less reliance on services, with an estimated cost reduction over their lifetime of up to £1000,000.

6

TRANSITIONS AND HOUSING

INTRODUCTION

All young people approaching adulthood are likely to want to explore the possibility of living more independently in the future, although some may be ready earlier than others to leave the family home. The same is true of those young people with physical and learning disabilities; however, their circumstances, the needs of their carers, or local housing provision may dictate the pace of this process. Provision of appropriate housing is likely to be a key feature in planning for a person's transition into adulthood, and should be considered early on as part of the transition reviews.

This chapter explores a variety of housing options and models that can be used with young people with disabilities, highlighting the challenges faced by transition workers when accessing them, and giving tips to improve the transition process.

LEGISLATIVE BACKGROUND

There have been a number of significant changes in policy and legislation that have sought to address some of the issues and challenges facing young people with disabilities.

In 2001, the government White Paper, *Valuing People,* highlighted the lack of choice for people with learning disabilities about where they live and with whom. It made clear recommendations about the need for housing and social services departments to work together to expand care and support options, and for local authorities to provide accessible advice and information. Independent living is featured throughout the White Paper as it is considered a good practice model to deliver more personalised services to people with learning disabilities, to enable them to have greater choice and control over their lives. This theme continued further in the government circular, *Putting People First* (DH 2010b), and in *Valuing People Now* (DH 2009a), where greater emphasis was placed on ensuring that mainstream housing policies are inclusive to people with learning disabilities. There was recognition that partnership boards were needed to consider how housing could be provided within the local area to meet the needs of people with learning disabilities.

The Localism Act 2011 was introduced to give responsibility back to local authorities in terms of planning and allocating housing, to ensure that key decisions are made locally. The guidance made clear that:

> In framing their allocation scheme to determine allocation priorities, housing authorities must ensure that reasonable preference is given to 'people who need to move on medical or welfare grounds, including grounds relating to a disability'. (DCLG 2012, p.17)

Further to establishing equality in housing for people with disabilities, the Disability Discrimination Act 2005 states that private landlords have an obligation to not treat those with disabilities less favourably, and from December 2006, both private and social landlords had new duties to provide reasonable adjustments for people with disabilities, as do those who control or manage rented property.

There is a wealth of policy and legislation that promotes the aspiration of independent living for people with disabilities, not all of which are included here. Despite this high-profile agenda, however, there remains a significant challenge, both to young people and those working with them, in planning for and securing appropriate housing.

REASONS FOR LEAVING HOME

A report by Mencap (2012) identifies that most people with learning disabilities want to live independently, although 38 per cent are living with family carers. The development of self-advocacy groups and the promotion of disability rights have been instrumental in empowering young people to make their own decisions, including about where they wish to live. When a young person makes the decision to leave home, it is imperative that the involved transition worker has time to explore their reasons, ensuring that they have capacity and fully understand the decision they are making. In some situations the parents of these young people may have differing views and want the young person to remain at home. Consideration of independent advocacy for the young person can help resolve these conflicts.

The decision to leave home and to live independently should be dictated by the young person where possible; however, there will be circumstances where alternative accommodation may be required from the age of 18. Those circumstances include young people in foster care whose placement will end at 18, and young people at residential schools and families who feel that they can no longer continue caring for a child once the consistent support of school comes to an end. Many young people without disabilities live with their families much longer than was previously the case, and so it is often thought that planning for housing when young people with disabilities are still at school is too early (DH 2011). Conversely, Read, Clements and Ruebain (2006) suggest it is crucial that as a young person approaches adulthood, steps are taken to look at what their needs are, and to work towards meeting them in a planned way. Therefore, whatever the reason for leaving home, transition planning needs to begin at an early stage to adequately prepare the young person and their family, and to manage their expectations realistically.

Changes to care arrangements can be especially difficult emotionally and practically for young people with disabilities who are in foster care and who have been so for a number of years. Often the young person views their foster carers as parents. It is therefore essential that they are prepared early on for a move at 18 if their foster parents are unable to continue with the placement, as they are likely to experience great sadness and loss if they are unable to remain living with them into adulthood. Being a foster carer is both a rewarding job and a beneficial career, and some foster carers may wish to remain as foster carers, working with the children for both personal and financial reasons. This needs to be handled sensitively by the workers supporting the young person through transition, with consideration given to how the young person can maintain contact, and be introduced to new accommodation and support services.

Placement termination is inevitable for children in residential schools, where a young person is usually required to leave no later than the academic year in which they are 19. If a young person remains in their residential school placement post-18, adult services will need to negotiate with both children's services and education around funding responsibility for continuation of the placement. Until recently, there was an argument that as children's services and education had developed the care plan with education needs being met at the school, they should continue to fund the plan until the young person's education finished. In reality, it is likely that adult services will need to pick up the social care costs and the entire package be shared between education and social care. The cost of placements in out of authority schools is high and steeply increasing (Audit Commission 2007), and it is beneficial to consider early on if a young person should remain at the school post-18 to finish their education. Where young people continue to make educational progress, and the social care element of the placement is meeting their care and support needs, assessments are likely to conclude that it is in the young person's best interests to remain in the placement to finish their education.

Caring for a young person with a disability can be mentally and physically demanding, and challenging behaviour in children with learning disabilities can lead to adverse effects in a sibling within the family (Gates and Atherton 2007). Consequently, some parents feel unable to continue post-18 for a variety of reasons. They may be worried about what will be offered in terms of support when the young person turns 18, wish to devote time to their other children, or feel that 18 is a natural time for young people to move on. Sometimes parents articulate their wish to regain their own life, to return to employment, or simply to make alternative arrangements while they feel able to. Local authorities may seek to discourage parents from making the decision to cease caring responsibilities due to the obvious financial pressures of providing alternative support, arguing that not all non-disabled young people move out of the family home at 18. This is true, of course, but many may go away to university around this time, or move in with friends, and almost all will no longer be dependent on their family for everyday support. It can also be argued that providing alternative care and support arrangements in a planned and structured way could enable young people to improve their independent living skills, and prevent a need for costly emergency placements, should the carer reach crisis in the future.

Transition workers need to be skilled in completing carer's assessments, and must ensure that each caring relationship is assessed on its individual circumstances without pre-judgement of difficult decisions made by family carers. Where a transition worker has been involved with a family for a number of years, this assessment and negotiation process is more effective, and enables the young person, carers and the worker to work together to consider future housing needs. With the right support and information, parents may feel more reassured about keeping the young person at home – knowing that they will be able to access short breaks and support when they need it may be enough for them not to consider alternative accommodation.

It should be acknowledged that there will be occasions where planning is not possible, and young people will require alternative accommodation in an emergency as a result of family breakdown, or removal from the family home under child protection/Court of Protection action as a result of abuse or neglect. In such circumstances the importance of having a transition worker who knows the young person is evident, as it can make the assessment process swifter, and housing needs easily identifiable.

In all of the above scenarios, the young person and their parents/carers will need to consider alternative housing options as early as possible, and young people want accessible information given directly to them rather than their parents (Morris 1999), to enable them to make an informed decision. However, as Dean (2003) argues, young people with disabilities rely on parents and care professionals for advice and guidance, but often these advisers know little about the housing and support choices available.

Transition workers need a good base knowledge of housing options for young people, and should be aware of where to access information. Providing good quality information early on around options, establishing an indicative budget, and considering who the young person wishes to live with will all support the young person and their families to identify what is a suitable, realistic and achievable housing model for them. Although there is an acknowledgement by most local authorities that by getting the right housing and support options for young people with disabilities the council could save significant amounts of money and reduce its dependency on residential care, liaising with housing providers, being creative with housing models and setting up shared supported living can be considerably time-consuming for social workers with already high caseloads. This has prompted some local authorities to do things differently. Dudley, for example, has an accommodation team that focuses on securing and moving people with disabilities into appropriate housing, and Northampton has recently appointed a commissioner for transition to look at the availability of housing and other services for young people in transition. In Worcestershire, the Young Adults Team has a housing project officer working at both a strategic and operational level to improve access to housing for young people with disabilities and taking on a project management role, working alongside social workers, to identify and negotiate supported living arrangements. Liaison with commissioners of housing services is essential to improve the quality of housing options in the future, and now accurate financial forecasting, based on a good understanding within adult social care of the numbers, needs and aspirations of young people coming through transition, is more essential than ever (Jarratt 2012).

TRANSITION PRACTITIONER TIPS

- Ensure that you seek the views separately of young people and their families about future living arrangements. Understanding their expectations early on can help you to plan effectively and manage any potential conflicts.

- Consider ways you can feed information about potential accommodation needs to commissioners and budget holders, ensuring that there is sufficient time to plan for forthcoming accommodation needs, and to accurately reflect potential future costings.

- Develop a tracking system to assist with financial forecasting.

CASE STUDY – TRANSITION PANEL

The Young Adults Team in Worcestershire recognised that a successful transition into alternative accommodation is dependent on many factors, and requires the input of other departments and organisations. It is important to recognise that no matter how planned and efficient your input as a team or transition worker may be, a transition can still be delayed if other key partners don't play their part. Taking this into consideration, the Young Adults Team developed the transition panel. The idea is for all transition workers to have a full day meeting to discuss the needs of all young people transitioning over the coming year. The meeting was predominantly designed to inform commissioners (who are invited to attend) about the numbers of young people requiring accommodation in the next year, what their specific accommodation needs are, and what their budgets are likely to be. This gives commissioners and the housing project officer the opportunity to commission appropriate services or to work with local housing and support providers. In addition, they were able to use one-page profiles to identify young people who wished to share with others.

On the whole, these meetings have been extremely successful, and have served not only as a platform for resolving housing issues, but also for addressing other transition issues. For example, at the last meeting a representative from the community nursing team and continuing healthcare (CHC) attended, and this enabled early identification of young people who may be eligible for CHC. As with all meetings, they can only be effective when all relevant parties attend, and therefore a commitment from all agencies to attend is essential.

Bringing workers together in this way has proved invaluable for sharing knowledge and raising issues. The scope of the transition panel could be much bigger and more effective. For example, it could include finance departments who could get accurate information about budgets etc. It could include funding panel decision-makers in order for indicative budgets to be agreed early on and support a well-planned transition, and, as Jarratt (2012) identified, successful and efficient transition processes have led to greater accuracy and confidence in financial forecasting. This has, in turn, focused attention on better transition practice, such as avoiding out of authority placements and residential care, and imaginative personalised solutions for young people identified as high cost.

HOUSING OPTIONS

Many young people identify that they do not wish to live alone at this stage of their life, and this is not unique to the disabled community. For this reason, shared tenancies and supported living are a popular choice. This option is not only beneficial in meeting the needs of the young person, but is favoured by councils promoting choice and control, looking at ways of maximising financial contributions from other sources. The Disability Rights Commission defines independent living as:

> ...all disabled people having the same choice, control and freedom as any other citizen – at home, at work, and as members of the community.

This does not necessarily mean disabled people 'doing everything for themselves', but it does mean that any practical assistance people need should be based on their own choices and aspirations. (cited in Human Rights Joint Committee 2012)

Young people with disabilities should have the same access to social housing as their non-disabled peers. Learner (2013) suggests that a lack of specialist housing, coupled with prejudice and misconceptions, is preventing people with learning disabilities living independently – and the situation is worsening. Young people are able to register on the local authority housing list to bid for properties when available, and for some young people living alone, with lower-level needs and without significant physical disabilities, this could be a realistic option. Many of the properties that are available are smaller, often one-bedroom flats. However, long waiting lists and points systems will sometimes prevent them securing local housing quickly, particularly if they still live at home, as they will not be deemed a priority on the list. Although those more cognitively and physically able may be able to secure this type of accommodation, they may have particular vulnerabilities in social housing. This is true of young people with Asperger's syndrome or high-functioning autism, where their uniqueness may draw attention to them in local communities and accommodation is in less desirable locations. Beadle-Brown *et al.* (2013) identify that those with lower support needs were more likely to be the victims of crime and to have been bullied. Transition workers supporting young people will need to ensure that they liaise with the housing authority to explain the young person's difficulties and vulnerabilities.

Securing local authority housing for young people with significant physical disabilities and who wish to share with others can be especially problematic, perhaps even impossible. Given the demands of social housing already, adapted properties or those suitable for young people to share do not often become available. Social care has tried to work more closely with housing services to establish ways of working more collaboratively to meet the needs of young people with disabilities, and while there are examples of this happening, they are the exception to the rule.

Private renting can offer a solution for young people with physical disabilities and those with more complex needs who wish to share with others. This option can give greater choice and flexibility of properties and areas, and may encourage landlords to consider a more long-lasting tenancy agreement. Many young people and their families raise concerns over private renting for a number of reasons, however, including the uncertainty that comes with a private tenancy that only lasts six to twelve months, which can make life difficult to plan and is often unsettling and a cause of worry (Patrick 2014). While it is now accepted that people are unlikely to remain in the same property for all of their lives, multiple moves, or those at short notice, are likely to have a significant impact on a young person with complex disabilities. It is therefore essential that the landlord is aware of the needs of the young people early on, and can work with a local authority to ensure that tenancies can be as long-term as possible. Educated landlords will welcome the prospect of having reliable tenants on a long-term basis.

The Welfare Reform Act 2012 is changing the way housing options are funded for people with disabilities, and impacts on local authorities' ability to support independent living. It places greater emphasis on people with high-level needs, and it is possible that those with less significant needs will not have access to the appropriate level of benefits that makes living independently achievable. With this in mind, consideration must be given early on in the transition planning process to the affordability of private renting – for example, will Housing Benefit cover the cost of the room, and where will any top-up come from? (See Appendix 1 for information on benefits.)

Raising these concerns early on and discussing the realities of housing options as early as the 14+ review can encourage young people and their families to consider how they can improve their chances of securing independent living in the future. There may be situations where family members would be willing to purchase a property and rent to their relative and other young people, or have access to a family or trust fund. Arranging this can be a complex process, and families are likely to require the support of housing associations such as, for example, Golden Lane Housing or Advance, and support from social care to achieve this. Shared ownership has become a popular concept in both the disabled and non-disabled population, as a means of allowing young people to get on the property ladder. Despite the help available around buying or shared ownership, only 2.5 per cent of people with learning disabilities own or partly own their own home (Mencap 2012). Options for renting a property are now more widely considered to be the best route for people with disabilities.

In order to hold a tenancy, young people will be required to sign a tenancy agreement. Tenancy agreements set out the young person's rights and responsibilities, alongside details of rent, liabilities, and so on. Understanding the details of a tenancy agreement can be complex for those without additional needs, and therefore those with disabilities will need support to interpret and understand a tenancy agreement. Many housing associations or private renting organisations provide easy read tenancy agreements. Those working with the young person will need to assess their capacity to understand the tenancy agreement before they allow them to sign it. As with all capacity assessments, it is essential that the worker uses appropriate communication methods, and where it is considered that a young person lacks capacity to sign a tenancy agreement, an application should be made to the Court of Protection for someone else to sign it on their behalf. This is a relatively straightforward process, and guidance and the appropriate forms can be found on the Court of Protection website.[1]

One of the most popular choices to provide supported living to people with disabilities is in small group homes, where housing is provided by a housing association or private letting agency. In this situation, two or more young people will share a property, each renting a room and holding individual tenancies. This can be a useful option in allowing friends to live together, and those with physical disabilities to have access to similar adaptations.

Within the true meaning of supported living, the landlord and care provider should be separate, and the young person should be able to maintain their tenancy and change their support provider as they wish. In reality, this is not always possible, and although they may have a legal and binding tenancy agreement, their home operates more like a traditional residential care service, where a care provider runs the home and commissioners 'place' people in their home (NDTi 2010). Living alone for those with high-level needs who have 24-hour care and support needs is an expensive option, and not currently widely achievable with the budgets allocated to young people. Sharing core hours of support, for example, waking night (where a member of staff is awake in the property) or sleep-in (where a member of staff sleeps over at the property), can be a useful way of meeting needs as well as reducing costs. However, budgets can only be shared when using

---

1   See www.gov.uk/court-of-protection.

the same provider, restricting the young person's choice and control around who supports them.

Developing these types of services can be both time-consuming and complicated. Workers will not only need to establish if young people are compatible to share, but will also need to consider if they are financially able to access this service. Practical consideration also needs to be given to the equipment, furniture and access to transport required. Within the Worcestershire Young Adults Team, the housing project officer, with assistance from transition workers, takes responsibility for identifying young people with similar needs who may wish to share. He then negotiates with providers around suitable properties and levels of support.

For young people with physical disabilities, moving into their own property can be dependent on access/equipment required, and a shortage of wheelchair-accessible housing is still a major barrier to independent living for those with mobility requirements (Morris 1999). When not accessing residential care, people with disabilities should have access to the equipment they need from the community occupational therapists. However, there can be lengthy waiting lists and difficulties in transferring equipment that may delay the process. Individuals can apply for grants to access adaptations, and there is no doubt that it would be more cost-effective for young people to share adaptations where possible; however, as Learner (2013) identifies in her article about the prejudice faced by tenants with learning disabilities and the lack of suitable housing, it would help if local authorities made grants available to people who needed to share accommodation.

CASE STUDY – LAUREN

Lauren is 18 years old and has profound and multiple learning disabilities (PMLD) and significant physical disabilities. She previously lived at home with her parents and siblings, but they are now struggling to manage her care and complex health needs at home. Lauren is a wheelchair user and requires a range of assistive technology and equipment to ensure her physical and health needs are met on a daily basis. This includes a specialist shower trolley, bed and hoist.

Given Lauren's complex health needs and need for 24-hour support and supervision, a single tenancy would have been very costly. In addition, it would not offer Lauren the opportunity to interact with a number of other people as she currently does at home, and her family feel that she would be socially isolated living alone with support.

Using one-page profiles, the housing project officer and social workers were able to identify three young women with complex physical disabilities all requiring accommodation. There was the opportunity for the young women to meet beforehand and to spend time together to ensure their compatibility for sharing a property. Once a property and support provider had been identified, it was necessary to not only consider the individual needs of the young people, but also what they would require collectively. For example, each young person had their own equipment needs to manage their personal care, and with only one bathroom in the property, consideration was needed around which equipment would be best suited to meet the needs of all three women. This kind of compromising and comparison proved particularly problematic, as each young woman had a different occupational therapist because they lived in different areas.

The housing project officer worked hard to negotiate with the existing occupational therapists for one person to take over the management of the three girls' occupational therapy assessments, and to request shared funding for equipment to meet all the needs. While it is evident that this is a useful approach to sharing equipment and reducing costs, it should be recognised that breaking down existing barriers and processes to achieve this was very time-consuming, and delayed the move for several months.

What this case study demonstrates are the difficulties faced in developing bespoke supported living services and the need for a coordinator to manage each individual project. Without the input of the housing project officer, transition workers with already high caseloads would have struggled to coordinate a project such as this, which resulted in positive outcomes, both for the young people concerned, and for the local authority.

SHARED LIVES SERVICES

Young people can find moving away from family daunting, particularly if it is into residential care or supported living placements that include a large staff team. Shared Lives offers an alternative: living with an individual or family who have signed up to become carers (Hardy 2014). Shared Lives placements can provide a more gradual move to independence for young people, and could be particularly useful when moving out of foster care. Adult placement and Shared Lives schemes enable young people to live with a carer in the carer's home. This ordinary family setting can be a good stepping-stone when moving into independence. Most schemes are provided under the supported living umbrella, and offer 24-hour support, with access to social security benefits. Used well, this service specification can improve the skills of young people, and equip them for more independent living in the future. It should be acknowledged, however, that young people may form an attachment to their carer, and may not wish to move on from that service. If the Shared Lives placement is to be used to increase independence, and is not seen as a permanent placement, discussion with the provider and the young person should make this clear during the support planning process. Support plans will need to identify outcomes around improving independence, and these should be reviewed regularly.

Shared Lives offers a cost-effective service and can provide a variety of flexible and personalised services for a wide range of individuals, including (with effective advance planning and care management support) those with highly complex needs (Fiedler 2006), although they are usually restricted to those with lower-level/moderate needs. Those with complex needs or challenging behaviour may not fit easily into this service. Early identification of a Shared Lives provider is invaluable in facilitating a transition process. It would allow for the young person to spend time with the new carer before any move takes place, minimising disruption and increasing the chances of placement success.

Converting to become a Shared Lives carer is a popular choice for foster carers who wish to continue to care for a child with disabilities post-18, and carers receive an allowance similar to foster carers, for each user, and can cater for needs that would not be met in a traditional care setting (Jackson 2010). Consultation with the young person, assessment of their capacity to decide where they wish to live, and consideration of what may be in their best interests needs thorough assessment well before a young person's eighteenth birthday. The foster carer will need detailed information about the Shared Lives scheme, how to register, and what is involved. The young person will require accessible information about how the arrangement differs now they are adults.

Situations are likely to arise where a young person was placed in foster care by another authority, and this can create confusion around who is responsible for taking a lead on the transition process. Transition workers from the placing authority should take the lead in organising and monitoring the transition, but successful transition can only be achieved if the receiving authority is involved in this process too, as the young person is likely to be considered to be ordinarily resident in that authority when they turn 18. The Care Act 2014 states that local authorities *must* assess a child prior to 18 if it considers there is significant benefit to the individual to do so, and requires them to continue to provide them with support services throughout the transition process. This is designed to remove the 'cliff edge' scenario, described by some young people where children's services just stop at 18. Under the Act, the receiving authority has responsibility for assessing the young person before they leave foster care, and the placing authority has responsibility for continuing funding the foster placement until new adult arrangements are in place. Post-foster care options could feature as part of the EHC plan outlined within the Children and Families Act 2014. The Care Act 2014 and SEN provisions in the Children and Families Act 2014 gives local authorities a legal responsibility to cooperate, and to ensure that all the right people work together to get transition right.

CLUSTER FLAT MODEL

There is increasing popularity within local authorities for the use of 'cluster flats'. This model is based on extra care housing, and young people have their own self-contained flat with individual support hours and access to communal areas. This type of housing is often suitable for people who want to live more independently than in a home, but have other people around to socialise with (Maxwell and King 2006). For young people this is an encouraging model that enables them to have independence while not feeling socially isolated. For those with very high-level needs, this can be a very expensive service, reducing the feasibility of access to it. However, this model should not be dismissed for those young people who may display aggressive and challenging behaviour and need their own space. There is the potential to provide one-to-one support with a background staff available, reducing costs and the level of staff intensity for the young person.

RESIDENTIAL CARE

Local authorities across the country are closely monitoring the ongoing use of residential care, particularly for young people. Most councils will have performance targets to reduce the number of people in residential care, and to increase those who have access to supported/independent living. A report by the Joseph Rowntree Foundation (Morris 2002) suggested that young people with high levels of support needs often move into residential or nursing care as they reach adulthood, and sometimes have little or no contact with young people of their own age. Furthermore, recent high-profile neglect/abuse cases, such as Winterbourne View, have reinforced this negative view of residential establishments, giving further weight to the idea of independent living.

While no one would argue with the increased choice and control offered by supported living, it needs to be recognised that it is not always achievable for those with complex health needs and/or challenging behaviour. For these young people, existing residential services can offer an appropriate environment and level of support to meet their needs, and sometimes at a more cost-effective price. It could be argued that looking at residential options for young people with disabilities offers a more balanced view of how their needs could be met. It may enable workers to challenge preconceptions about support services from parents and family members, and aid in expelling some of the myths they may hold around supported/ independent living. Discounting residential care altogether as an option could be as oppressive as only considering that option. Transition planning needs to take into account the needs and wishes of the young person, and on a few occasions those needs and wishes could still best be met in a residential service.

One major disadvantage associated with residential care is the likelihood that the young person would have to slot into an existing group of people who may not be of a similar age or have similar interests. Developing small group supported living services gives the opportunity for young people to have a say in who they wish to share a home with and the opportunity to see if they get on beforehand. Young people with disabilities, particularly those with communication or challenging behaviour, often find it difficult to make and maintain friendships with others. As a result, they may not naturally be able to identify a friend or group of friends they wish to live with. In circumstances where young people do have friends they wish to live with, the person-centred planning process can be useful in identifying this, and considering housing options to meet those young people's needs.

Self-advocacy/support groups will often provide a matching service. This will involve young people completing a profile about their interests, where they wish to live, and so on, and attending social events to get to know each other. Some local authorities will facilitate this too, using one-page profiles. Workers will use their knowledge of young people to match those with similar interests or levels of need. A word of caution is needed in relation to this approach, however, as although people have similar care needs or similar interests on paper, it does not necessarily mean that they will get on with each other. This can also be true of age. We assume that young people wish to live with other young people, and while this is generally the case, there are situations where people of different ages with similar interests may be an equally appropriate match.

By enabling young people to meet on several occasions and where possible, have overnight respite stays together, there is a greater likelihood that they will be suited to live with each other, and it is less likely that any future placement will break down. The involved transition worker should consider early on during the assessment process with whom the young person may wish to live and any close friendships they may identify. Friends and relationships are important issues for young people, but transition planning, assessments and services rarely address these concerns (Morris 2002).

TRANSITION PRACTITIONER TIPS

- Encourage young people and their carers to think early on about what their future accommodation plans may be.

- Consider where you can access appropriate information about housing options, and encourage young people to explore these with their family if they are thinking of leaving home in the future. Look at whether information on housing options is published as part of the Local Offer.

- Meet with commissioners and senior management, and ask for support to coordinate supported living projects or query with your line manager how this could be done as part of the transition process. Find out how they convey the housing needs of young people coming through transition to prospective providers.

- Encourage all young people you work with to complete a one-page profile, and find out about support offered by local advocacy services for matching up people to share accommodation.

- Identify a link within local housing to establish support with access to social housing.

- Consult regularly with the Shared Lives scheme and consider raising the profile of Shared Lives within transition events and carers groups.

CONCLUSION

This chapter has addressed some of the reasons behind young people leaving the family home and recognises the importance of young people exploring all housing opportunities available to them. Having access to straightforward information that supports them to make realistic decisions about their future is pivotal for young people to consider the possibility of leaving home.

This chapter has recognised how difficult it can be for transition workers working in isolation to access a wide range of housing options and that despite the variety of housing options available to young people with disabilities, they continue to face greater challenges to identify and access suitable housing than their non-disabled peers, as a result of lower expectations and practical barriers including a lack of adapted property.

Without the input of those responsible for commissioning services and strong links with housing providers, development of shared and supported living will be severely hindered, workers will be unable to be as creative as they would like, and there is the potential for further dependency on existing residential placements.

What this chapter demonstrates is the challenge faced by workers supporting young people to not only access suitable housing but to achieve this within current budget constraints and limited housing stock. Despite the challenges raised in this chapter it is essential that all transition workers recognise that young people have a right to live as independently as possible, whatever housing model is used to achieve this.

RESOURCES

For information on the Court of Protection, see: *www.gov.uk/court-of-protection.*

For information around Shared Lives, see Shared Lives Plus: *www.sharedlivesplus.org.uk.*

For general information around housing options for young people with disabilities, see the Foundation for People with Learning Disabilities: *www.learningdisabilities.org.uk.*

For information on shared ownership, purchasing property and supported living options, see:

Golden Lane Housing: *www.glh.org.uk.*

Advance: *www.advanceuk.org.*

Housing and Support Alliance: *www.housingandsupport.org.uk.*

Housing and Support Alliance: *www.housingandsupport.org.uk/shared-ownership-homebuy-and-hold.*

7

TRANSITIONS AND HEALTH

INTRODUCTION

Our health is possibly *the* most important factor in enabling us all to live happy and fulfilled lives. For young people with disabilities, getting their health needs right can be the difference between a successful and unsuccessful transition into adulthood.

Young people with complex disabilities, health needs and life-limiting conditions are now living longer thanks to advances in medical technology, and it is of great importance that their potential needs in adult services are acknowledged and planned for, and that they are supported well throughout the transition process.

Those with physical or learning disabilities or both are likely at some point to require a number of medical interventions, ranging from access to mainstream healthcare such as GPs, dental care and so on, to specialist support from physiotherapy, occupational therapy and speech and language therapy. Some or all of these services will need to continue to be accessed in adult services. Within this chapter, specific health services important in transition are highlighted, and issues around challenging behaviour, mental health and sex and relationships are examined.

TRANSFER FROM PAEDIATRIC TO ADULT HEALTHCARE
FOR YOUNG PEOPLE WITH DISABILITIES

Young people and their carers generally view healthcare services throughout childhood as predictable and reliable. Relationships with healthcare professionals are usually consistent, and young people and their families have an understanding of what to expect. It can be argued that in the UK, however, adult disability services are in general still poorly developed in comparison to those provided for children (Lissouer and Clayden 2011), and that transition practitioners face a difficult challenge in supporting the transfer from paediatric to adult health services. Children with specific health conditions are likely to have a consultant paediatrician in addition to their GP, who will monitor their health needs throughout their childhood, and in some circumstances, paediatricians are linked to local special schools and provide regular surgeries there to ensure that they see all children regularly to monitor their development and condition. The reliance on the physical school building is evident when it comes to organising and monitoring healthcare services. Most special schools will have a school nurse on site to assist in monitoring day-to-day health needs, refer on for specialist input, and take a lead role in coordinating medical interventions. Some of these interventions include the following:

PHYSIOTHERAPY

Young people with physical disabilities such as cerebral palsy, muscular dystrophy and spina bifida will almost certainly encounter physiotherapy services in their childhood, with an emphasis on maximising and developing their mobility and maintaining their muscle tone. Specialist learning disability physiotherapists are a limited resource, and may not always be available within specialist adult services (Gates and Barr 2009). Transition workers will need to establish at their initial transition meeting and within their assessment if there is a continued need or recommendation for ongoing physiotherapy into adulthood, and where or how this can be accessed. In Community Learning Disabilities Teams, physiotherapists may be accessed via a referral to the team, and in some situations the children's physiotherapists may refer directly to their colleagues in adult services. Specialist equipment such as standing frames, chairs and walkers may be used in school, and it is essential to establish if these will move with the young person into their adult placement. Physiotherapists may also assess a need for specialist shoes/orthotics, and recommend a need for therapeutic activities such as hydrotherapy and rebound therapy. There may be less availability of these types of therapies in adult services, and having a clear understanding of why they are recommended is needed when transition planning.

OCCUPATIONAL THERAPY/EQUIPMENT

Support from an occupational therapist is frequently sought for young people with physical and learning disabilities, who are most likely to assess them for equipment they require to enable them to be as independent as possible. Equipment could include specialist beds, bathing aids, audio monitors and so on. For those with physical and mobility needs, they may require access to a wheelchair that needs to be regularly reviewed and re-assessed, and support to attend the wheelchair clinic regularly is likely to need to be continued into adulthood.

Young people with complex learning disabilities are more likely to have sensory issues, and poor behavioural organisation is often linked to sensory integration (Mednick 2002). Such difficulties can affect their tolerance to noise, touch and so on, and occupational therapists are skilled in completing in-depth sensory assessments to establish ways of working with the young person to minimise the distressed caused by the sensory difficulty. Transition practitioners will need to establish if the young person has an ongoing need for occupational therapy support, and refer on accordingly, particularly if a young person is intending to move into alternative accommodation. It is most likely that separate referrals will be required for specific occupational therapy input as specialist resources within adult services are limited, and input generally provided by generic occupational therapists as and when needed.

SPEECH AND LANGUAGE THERAPY

Speech and language support is arguably one of the most controversial services to be considered during the transition process as resources, again, can be significantly limited within adult services. Speech and language therapists are also likely to be linked with schools, and offer assessments around eating and drinking guidelines and communication methods. Many young people will have speech and language support within their Statement of SEN, but may not actually get this. With the introduction of the EHC plan, access to speech and language support is likely to change, and the Local Offer must also include speech and language therapy and other therapies such as physiotherapy, occupational therapy and services relating to mental health (Silas 2014).

Ongoing speech and language support in adults is also very rare, and may need to be referred to the Community Learning Disability Teams once a young person turns 18, but this is usually for a one-off piece of work such as an eating and drinking assessment. This can be difficult for young people and parents to adapt to, particularly as their communication needs, although not directly supported by a speech and language therapist, will have been a high priority within the school curriculum.

How a young person with a disability communicates should form the basis of any intervention or support offered to them, and it is essential that future support services are aware of the tools and methods they use. Creating a Communication Passport can be a useful tool to support transition between services. Its point is to capture the unique and sometimes subtle or idiosyncratic ways an individual communicates (Atherton and Crickmore 2011).

PSYCHOLOGY AND PSYCHIATRY

Access to clinical psychology and psychiatry may become necessary as young people experience adolescence and struggle to manage the change in hormones and feelings. For young people with learning disabilities, these changes may prompt alterations in behaviour that could become problematic, both towards themselves and others. Where psychology or psychiatry support is already in place through children's services, consideration needs to be given to how this will continue if needed in adult services. Referring for psychology or psychiatry support can be a useful way to ensure young people are supported to manage risks towards themselves and others.

TRANSITION PRACTITIONER TIPS

- Prior to or during the transition review, ask for contact information and details of all health professionals involved with the young person, and make a note of any ongoing health conditions and input that is required.

- Ask for the school nurse to attend reviews where possible, as they may have a vital role to play in engaging health professionals and supporting the transition process. Consider scheduling quarterly meetings with the school nurse to flag up any health issues for young people approaching transition. This may not be achievable if you work with a number of special schools, however.

- Find out what internal processes exist for transferring referring to adult therapy services. Do therapists do this automatically, or should the young person be referred only when a specific issue occurs?

USING THE TRANSITION/EHC PLAN REVIEW

With such a predictable system and familiar environment as a child, it is little wonder that young people find the notion of transferring from children's to adult services somewhat daunting. In a report produced by the Care Quality Commission, a parent described the process of moving from paediatric to adult healthcare as 'from the pond, you are picked up and put in the sea' (CQC 2014). Greater coordination between children's and adult healthcare services is needed if young people are to achieve a successful transition, and for young people with EHC plans, it should be the basis for coordinating the integration of health with other services (Silas 2014). Royal College of Nursing guidance around adolescent and transition care (RCN 2013) states that transition planning should begin from the age of 13 to adequately prepare young people and their families, and to begin a health transition plan.

Discussions around who will be lead practitioners to support the young person in transition need to happen at the earliest opportunity. A transition review at age 14+ or the EHC plan review provides the best platform to start this process. Too often, however, these reviews can be tokenistic, education-focused, and cover only surface information, as it can be too early to effectively plan for transition at this stage. There is a real opportunity here to identify who will take a lead on coordinating healthcare and assigning individual responsibilities to involved professionals. It should be noted that not all services will end at 18, and in health services this can vary from one department to another. In the majority of cases, where a young person receives therapies and paediatric care via the school, this support will remain in place potentially up to the age of 19 when they leave school; the point of transition to adult services may therefore vary for each individual.

CASE STUDY – FRED

Fred is 17 years old and will be leaving school next year, but turns 18 in three months' time. Fred has a severe learning disability, no verbal communication, and displays sexually inappropriate behaviour that is now impacting on his ability to access the community safely. In addition, Fred has increased anxiety around medical interventions such as going to the dentist and seeing his paediatrician.

Fred's health issues were raised by the school nurse during his annual education review. The nurse had regular contact with Fred's paediatrician who has known Fred for many years, and undertakes his appointments with him at school to minimise his anxiety. Fred is also visited at school by a dentist and optician, when required. It was identified during the review that Fred has a complex set of health needs, and in order for there not to be an increase in his challenging behaviour and a risk to others, careful planning is needed to ensure his health needs continue to be met as an adult. Several recommendations were made in the review:

- Fred's behaviour at school and in the community is becoming very problematic and he is a risk to himself and others. It was recommended that Fred be referred to an adult psychiatrist and psychologist to consider how to respond appropriately to his over-sexualised behaviour.

- The occupational therapist agreed to review the equipment used to support Fred in the community to ensure his safety and the safety of others. She agreed that she would refer directly to the adult occupational therapist if Fred required ongoing support when he left school.

- The speech and language therapist agreed to complete a Communication Passport to inform adult service staff of how best to communicate with Fred, and highlighted the importance of consulting with him in a familiar environment. She also agreed to refer directly to adult services if speech and language therapy services were needed when he left school.

- The school nurse agreed to refer Fred to the Adult Community Learning Disability Team for support from a community nurse to oversee and coordinate health appointments and to complete a Health Action Plan (HAP).

LEAD PROFESSIONALS AND THE ROLE OF COMMUNITY NURSES

Bridging the gap between paediatric and adult healthcare can be a challenge for workers supporting young people in transition, particularly when the majority of specialist transition workers have a social care background. Despite Department of Health guidance stating that where a young person has significant and complex health needs the lead professional should be a medical practitioner, the reality is that the majority of transitions are coordinated by social care staff. The Department of Health Partnerships for Children, Families and Maternity 2008 guidance, *Transition: Moving on Well*, states that a HAP needs to be developed by the young person, supported by the relevant health professional/transition key worker or another relevant multi-disciplinary team member who can review it with them regularly. Even though many Adult Community Learning Disability Teams tend to be integrated with both health and social care staff, it is not clear if this goes far enough in terms of transition. The role of the community nurse in learning disability services continues to evolve, and where it was originally viewed that their role should be carefully targeted at health-related activities as a first priority (DH 2007a), they are now more frequently taking on a care management role. While it could be argued that this reduces their ability to carry out health promotion work and health interventions, there is also an argument that they are best placed in some circumstances to support young people and plan their transition into adulthood. Transition teams/services that have both nurses and social workers are likely to have a wider bank of skills and resources to help support young people in transition, and learning disability nurses can ensure that young people have up-to-date HAPs and receive annual health checks in addition to providing specialist liaison to mainstream services such as GPs. Community social work or Physical Disability Teams will not have the same level of integration with health as Community Learning Disabilities Teams, and this can make coordination of a transition for young people with physical disabilities more difficult.

SPECIFIC HEALTH ISSUES FOR PEOPLE WITH LEARNING DISABILITIES

Young people with learning disabilities frequently have additional health needs to those of their non-disabled peers. There is a particularly high prevalence of epilepsy in the learning disabled population (Baker and Jacoby 2000), and specialist epilepsy pathways and additional resources are often available to help support young people and their families to manage the condition appropriately. Most health authorities will have specialist epilepsy nurses who can be involved in transition planning and offer specialist training to adult providers. *Valuing People* (DH 2001) identified that most people with learning disabilities have greater health needs than the rest of the population, and that mainstream health services have been slow in developing the capacity and skills to meet the needs of people with learning disabilities. The White Paper introduced the notion of every person with a learning disability having a health facilitator and their own HAP by 2005. A health facilitator does not need to be a nurse – they can be a parent, friend, support worker, or key worker (Evans and Tippins 2008).

HAPs are designed to be working documents that are owned and kept by the person with a learning disability. They should hold all essential information about the young person's health appointments and contact details for healthcare providers such as GPs, dentists and so on. Having a HAP can prove effective, both in monitoring someone's health, and in identifying which healthcare services and professionals are needed to make sure people have the support they need to stay healthy (Hardie and Tilly 2012). Most local authorities will have their own HAP format; however, it should be recognised that this may need to be adapted or changed, depending on that young person's communication needs. Having a HAP will be irrelevant if all those working with that young person are not aware of its existence or are not actively using it. The ambiguity around whose responsibility it is to complete a HAP could result in a delay in one being developed for the young person. Having health action planning as a set agenda item to discuss at the 14+ transition/EHC plan review is one way of addressing this. While it would be considered too early at this stage to be compiling the plan, a lead facilitator can be identified to take on this responsibility in the future. Consideration should also be given to whether the HAP could be incorporated into the EHC plan to prevent duplication of information.

With the advancement in medical technology and increasing awareness and understanding of complex conditions, young people with life-limiting and complex needs are now living longer, and those who were thought unlikely to make it into adult services are doing so with a very complex set of needs. Those with complex learning disabilities and physical disabilities are often described as having profound and multiple learning disabilities (PMLD). A characteristic of the support needed by this cohort of young people is a heavier reliance on medical intervention. This could include things such as not being able to maintain body temperature, unstable and unpredictable epilepsy, breathing difficulties and so on. In situations where someone with PMLD has a variety of health needs, they are also likely to require consideration for CHC funding, and transition workers can be trained to identify when someone will potentially require a CHC assessment as they enter adulthood.

CASE STUDY – LEO

Leo is a 16-year-old young man with PMLD. He lives at home with his parents and receives a 24-hour support package to manage his deteriorating health needs and complex epilepsy. Although Leo attends a special school, his attendance is sporadic due to the severity of his epilepsy and a constant need to adapt his care and medication regime. His package of support at home is currently provided by health and social services, and he is supported by workers from a nursing agency and through workers recruited as PAs under direct payments.

A school review was arranged at 16 to make plans for Leo's transition, and all those involved with his care were invited to attend. Although chaired by the head teacher, the review had a specific focus around Leo's post-school and post-18 care. It was identified that although Leo could remain at school until 19, this was no longer benefiting him as he was frequently unable to attend, and although he gained from the social interaction, his medical condition was making him increasingly sleepy, and he often needed to sleep following seizures for several hours a day. Therefore identification of what Leo would do at 18 and who would fund his care was required. Actions from the review included the following:

- The transition worker would work alongside Leo's family, the school, specialist nurse and all those involved in supporting him to complete a personal assessment under the NHS and Community Care Act 1990.

- The specialist nurse would work alongside Leo and his family to produce a HAP and establish how his therapeutic services would continue when he left school. This involved liaison with physiotherapy, speech and language therapy and occupational therapy.

- The currently involved specialist nurse would complete a CHC checklist alongside Leo and his family to establish if he met the eligibility for a full CHC assessment, and refer this to the local CHC team no later than Leo's seventeenth birthday.

CONTINUING HEALTHCARE

CHC funding is a pot of money that has a specific set of rules. In order for a young person with a disability to access it, they must have a 'primary health need' (DH 2012). Although funding from health is also available for someone as a child under the age of 18, the rules are quite different. Children's continuing care (under 18) involves a package of support from primary care trusts (PCTs), local authorities and other partners. Essentially this means that health may contribute to a package of support but they do not fund it entirely, as is the case with adult NHS CHC. CCGs should also ensure that adult NHS continuing healthcare is appropriately represented at all transition planning meetings concerning individual young people whose needs suggest that there may be potential eligibility. It suggests further that adult CHC teams should be notified early about young people at around the age of 14 who are potentially likely to be eligible for adult CHC when they turn 18. This would allow for tracking of the individual's needs, and a referral to complete the NHS CHC checklist at age 16. The guidance continues to state that at 17 a full CHC assessment should be completed as part of a multi-disciplinary process and eligibility determined. This would allow for CHC funding to be in place at 18 years and support a successful transition. Transition practitioners considering eligibility should be aware that those young people who were not eligible as children for CHC may be eligible as adults.

The CHC checklist and decision support tool should take place prior to full assessment of a young person's need for CHC, and can be completed by any professional who knows the young person well and has experience/ training in completing it. It is essential for all transition workers to have a level of understanding about the CHC checklist should they need to use it. Many young people with disabilities attend special schools and have a school nurse who has regular input in monitoring their health needs, and they can be useful partners to support completion of the checklist. Accessible information about the CHC checklist should be given to young people and their families early on in the transition process. The Foundation for People with Learning Disabilities has produced a useful guide called *What Do I Need to Know about Continuing Healthcare?* (Giraud-Saunders 2012), which provides detailed information about the CHC process. Those completing the checklist will also need to bear in mind the young person's capacity to consent to the checklist being completed. Where a person lacks capacity, a best interests decision should be completed.

Where the checklist indicates that a young person with disabilities has complex unstable health issues or behaviours, a full Continuing Healthcare assessment is required. For people with severe learning disabilities and challenging behaviour, management of their behavioural needs could be integral to ensuring successful transition planning. It is therefore essential for transition workers to recognise the importance of not only physical health conditions, but also a young person's cognition and behaviour in considering NHS CHC eligibility.

CHC ASSESSMENT

The completion of a CHC assessment should be a person-centred process that fully involves the young person and their family. The responsible primary care trust (PCT) (or clinical commissioning group, CCG) will need to identify a lead health professional to complete the assessment. For people with learning disabilities, this is likely to be a community nurse. The PCT or CCG responsible for completing the assessment is the placing area, even if the young person is currently placed in a different authority. The exception to this is if a young person was placed in their current placement prior to 2007. In this situation, this authority would be responsible for completing the CHC assessment. Although each authority works to CHC guidelines, it is likely that they will conduct the assessment and make decisions slightly differently in each authority.

Using existing available information about the young person, such as their community care assessment, speech and language reports, behaviour management plans and so on, the lead professional will bring together all relevant information about the young person to complete their assessment. Once the assessment is complete, it will be presented by the health professional at a CHC panel, where a decision around eligibility should be made.

Where a young person is deemed eligible for CHC funding, the health professional will take on the coordination and care management role, although it is likely that transition workers will continue to have a vital role to play as they will have been monitoring the needs of the young person and supporting them to look at adult options. Establishing links and developing transition processes with the local CHC team is essential to ensure that there is not a delay in assessing young people with complex health needs and developing person-centred support packages. Many authorities are now trialling personal health budgets (PHBs), and as of April 2014, PHBs became an established feature of the NHS (Alakeson 2014), meaning that anyone eligible for CHC funding is entitled to request one.

TRANSITION PRACTITIONER TIPS

- Familiarise yourself with the NHS CHC checklist/decision-making tool, and consider who may be appropriate to complete these for the young people you work with. There may be a school or community nurse involved who could assist you.

- Find out if training is offered by the PCT or elsewhere about the CHC process, and take part in this.

- Find out how you refer for CHC assessments. Is there a dedicated CHC nurse? Do you refer to Community Learning Disabilities Teams? Find out who is responsible for undertaking CHC assessments for people with physical disabilities.

- Meet with your local CHC team and ask them about developing a pathway/process for young people to be assessed prior to turning 18, as stated in CHC guidance.

- Ask for written information about the CHC assessment process, policy and complaints procedure in order for you to give this to the young people and families when you meet.

SEX AND RELATIONSHIPS

Adolescence is a difficult time for all young people. Feelings of confusion around their bodies changing, unfamiliar changes in hormones, and attractions towards others are difficult enough for the non-disabled population. For young people with disabilities this can prove bewildering. Friends and sexual relationships are important issues for young people, but transition planning, assessments and services rarely address these concerns (Morris 2002, p.4). For those young people who are heavily reliant on family for support, this can be a difficult area to discuss, and there is potential for conflicting views between the young person and their carers. Having access to appropriate and accessible sex education and information is imperative at this stage, and there are various resources to assist with this.

Facilitated peer group workshops can be a useful way of addressing some of these issues in a safe environment away from family members. These sessions can also be useful in addressing appropriate and inappropriate touch, as studies of adults with learning disabilities continue to show high levels of sexual abuse (Haaken and Reavey 2010).

For workers supporting young people, they have to strike a balance between a person's vulnerability and their right to take part in intimate relationships. The Mental Capacity Act 2005 can prove useful in protecting the young person and the worker involved in the case. It is difficult for us to accept sometimes that although a young person may make an unwise decision, they may not necessarily lack capacity. Young people all have to make their own mistakes and have the opportunity to take risks to enable them to better protect themselves.

CASE STUDY – DY10 NIGHTS

In 2004 a transition coordinator was appointed in Worcestershire to make links with the local community, to involve young people more in their transition, and to address access to leisure activities. Working with a small group of young people with learning disabilities, the coordinator identified a need for an accessible nightclub. People with learning disabilities desperately wanted to have the experience of going to a nightclub to dance, drink and meet people, but most advised that they felt vulnerable and at risk of ridicule by non-disabled youngsters. This lead to the development of the DY10 nightclub night.

With the support of the transition coordinator and advocacy group, a group of young people approached a local nightclub and negotiated that for one Monday each month, a club night would be put on for young people with disabilities. Essentially, the night should run like any other night. Alcohol would be sold freely, there would be door staff and a DJ, and it should offer the young people experience of clubbing in a potentially less vulnerable environment. For those who needed extra assistance, a carer was admitted free of charge, and volunteers from Connexions, social services, advocacy and voluntary groups attended as additional low-level support, such as making sure they could call for taxis and did not leave unsupported if they were unable to travel independently.

The night was a huge success, and continues to run today. There have been a variety of learning experiences for the young people who attend, including having too much to drink, arguments over 'who fancies who', established and long-lasting romances, and an ability to 'dance dirty' with someone without their parents watching.

What this case study demonstrates is that all young people, regardless of disability, want to have the opportunity to be young and to experiment with relationships. Having a model like DY10 means that they are able to do this in a more protected environment, having the same experiences, while limiting the risk of abuse and exploitation. The night is now entirely run by young people with the support of the self-advocacy group. This shows that if things are set up appropriately and with service user involvement, they are much more likely to be successful. Due to the identified issues around a lack of understanding of sex and relationships, the young people involved in DY10 were able to access some funding to provide two workers to run a daytime programme on sex and relationships using the nightclub as a base. Using age-appropriate resources and adapted information, these young people had an opportunity to talk about sex and their feelings in an appropriate way. In reality, for individual workers with a full caseload, their ability to set up initiatives like the one above is likely to be severely limited. However, it is worth workers finding out about similar projects in their area of work for them to direct young people to, or they could contact local self-advocacy groups and suggest they do something similar.

Such is the desire to have meaningful relationships that a dating agency for people with disabilities has been developed, and recently featured on the Channel 4 show, *The Undateables*. Stars in the Sky are an organisation that support young people with disabilities looking for love.

Used appropriately, social media such as Facebook can support young people to develop and maintain relationships with their peers. It enables young people to talk to each other and to stay in contact with boyfriends and girlfriends they may have met at college, for example. But this use of social media also has an element of risk attached to it, potentially exposing young people to grooming.

CASE STUDY – CHLOE

Chloe is a 17-year-old young woman with learning disabilities and attachment difficulties. She has displayed behaviour that has proved too challenging for her parents to continue caring for her at home, and lives in a children's residential placement. Chloe is independent in many ways, and has had a number of 'boyfriends'. She has recently befriended a 47-year-old man on Facebook, and has met with him on several occasions and has had sex in public parks with him. Chloe believes this man loves her and sees nothing wrong with the relationship; however, the staff at her placement are concerned about her vulnerability and sexual health safety. Chloe requested to live independently in her own flat when she leaves the children's residential unit at 18, but the transition worker understandably had concerns about her vulnerability. Alongside other areas of transition planning, the transition worker had to take into account the following issues:

- *Capacity*: using the Mental Capacity Act, the worker completed a capacity assessment and identified that although making an unwise decision, Chloe understood the risks concerned with having sex in a public place.

- *Education*: the transition worker identified that Chloe would benefit from further education around sex, protecting herself from infection. With her consent, the worker was able to refer Chloe to a specialist sexual health nurse experienced in working with people with learning disabilities.

- *Accommodation*: working closely with Chloe, the worker supported her to look at options that bridged a gap between a residential placement and independent living. Chloe moved into a Shared Lives placement which increased her independence, while continuing to ensure that she had daily support to improve her independence and self-protection skills.

- *Protection*: the worker consulted with the police and raised concerns about the appropriateness of the relationship. Giving them the man's contact details, she was able to establish that he had no prior convictions.

TRANSITION PRACTITIONER TIPS

- Find out what resources there are locally to support young people in exploring issues around sex. Could psychology or community nurses support with sex education?

- Consider what social opportunities are available for young people to meet others, such as Stars in the Sky.

- Where appropriate, ask young people their views around sex and relationships away from family, as they may be uncomfortable discussing this in front of them.

- Identify potential risks using risk assessments and the Mental Capacity Act to support your decision-making.

MENTAL HEALTH AND CHALLENGING BEHAVIOUR

Children and adolescents with learning disabilities are over six times more likely to have a diagnosable psychiatric disorder than their peers who do not have learning disabilities (BOND 2014). With this in mind, consideration of mental health issues needs to be an integral part of the assessment process. Young people with this dual diagnosis may already be receiving support from the Child and Adolescent Mental Health Service (CAMHS), and some may be accommodated or sectioned under the Mental Health Act 1983. CAMHS offer direct support to young people who may display violent or angry behaviour, depression, low self-esteem, eating disorders, obsessions or compulsions, anxiety, sleep problems, self-harming and the effects of abuse or traumatic events. Unfortunately CAMHS tends to have lengthy waiting lists, and at times social workers have found that there is a mismatch between their ideas and those of mental health professionals (Southall 2005). If CAMHS workers are involved with young people in transition, it is essential that they are invited to play an active role in EHC plan reviews and transition planning meetings. Asking them to support visits to prospective adult placements is also useful. Coordination of transition for people detained under the Mental Health Act is likely to be planned using the Care Programme Approach (CPA). This is a programme of assessment and care planning, where risk management, crisis and contingency planning are integral to the process (DH 2008). It is useful to have an understanding of this approach, and further information on supporting young people with mental health difficulties can be found in the Resources section below.

Planning transition for a young person with mental health issues and/or severely challenging behaviour is likely to be a huge challenge for transition workers, particularly in terms of identifying appropriate adult service provision within the agreed personal budget. Some authorities will have behaviour support services that work alongside young people, schools and families to identify ways to manage behaviour. Getting these workers identified and on board early on in the transition process is a useful way of supporting new providers in working with these young people. This cohort of young people are likely to require a more intense transition that looks at minimising anxiety and the likelihood that the behaviour will increase as a result of any move.

TRANSITION PRACTITIONER TIPS

- Identify early on how behaviour is managed. Are there existing behaviour management plans in place? Who were these completed by?

- Identify if the young person is being supported by specialist behaviour workers or CAMHS. Ensure these workers are invited to all transition meetings, and investigate if this support will continue post-18, and if not, who will take on this support in adult services.

- Attend training around Mental Health Act and CPA. Although it may not be frequently experienced, having a good knowledge base is essential should you be asked to work with someone detained under the Mental Health Act.

- Ensure that assessments of needs are completed at least twelve to six months prior to the young person leaving school/turning 18 to ensure there is sufficient time to identify funding and enable a lengthy transition.

CONCLUSION

This chapter has identified a range of health issues for young people with disabilities and highlights how transition workers will need to ensure that the health needs of young people feature throughout the assessment process. As literature and research around transition for young people with disabilities suggest, moving between paediatric and adult healthcare is frequently daunting and problematic for young people and their carers, particularly when a young person's health needs are complex and require specialist input. In addition it is recognised that access to some of these specialist healthcare services and resources often become more limited as young people enter adulthood.

In order to support young people in moving from the relative stability of paediatric into adult healthcare, a health facilitator should be identified early to coordinate this, making use of resources such as EHC plans and health action plans. However, despite the variety of resources around facilitating health transitions, it is clear that there remains a great deal of work to be done in engaging health services at the transition planning stage, and challenging them to take an active role in care management where it is appropriate.

Transition workers will need a good level of understanding about health services, guidance around Continuing Healthcare and specialist services for people with disabilities if they are to successfully challenge health services to take an active role in transition planning. Having a transition support service that included both health and social care professionals would go some way to ensuring that young people with complex health needs were supported appropriately through the transition process. However, there is also a need at a higher level for health and social care to establish how they can better work together to assess, fund and commission the right health services for young people with disabilities.

RESOURCES

For information around Communication Passports, see the Personal Communication Passports website: *www.communicationpassports.org.uk*.

For information around Health Action Plans (HAPs), see the Easyhealth website: *www.easyhealth.org.uk*.

For information on personal health budgets (PHBs), see: *www.personalhealthbudgets.england.nhs.uk*.

Stars in the Sky (a dating agency for people with learning difficulties): *www.starsinthesky.co.uk*.

For accessible information about sex and relationships, see the BILD website: *www.bild.org.uk*.

For information about the Care Programme Approach (CPA), see: *www.rethink.org/resources/c/care-programme-approach-cpafactsheet*.

For an overview of the Mental Health Act in relation to learning disabilities, see: *www.aboutlearningdisabilities.co.uk/overview-mental-health-act.html*.

For information about managing behaviour and supporting those with autism in transition, see the 'Autism toolkit' on the Autism Education website at: *www.autismeducationtrust.org.uk/resources/transition%20toolkit.aspx*.

DH (Department of Health) (2012) *National Framework for NHS Continuing Healthcare and NHS Funded Nursing Care*. London: The Stationery Office. Available at www.gov.uk/government/publications/national-framework-for-nhs-continuing-healthcare-and-nhs-funded-nursing-care.

Giraud-Saunders, A. (2012) *What Do I Need to Know about NHS Continuing Healthcare? Information for Families of People with Learning Disabilities*. London: Foundation for People with Learning Disabilities. Available at www.peoplehub.org.uk/9.pdf.

SCIE (Social Care Institute for Excellence) (2011) *Mental Health Service Transitions for Young People*. SCIE Guide 44. London: SCIE. Available at www.scie.org.uk/publications/guides/guide44/index.asp?dm_i=4O5,KTJ9,56SMOE,1OVUQ,1.

8

TRANSITIONS AND DECISION-MAKING

INTRODUCTION

Transition from childhood to adulthood is a time that can require multiple decisions, which may have implications and consequences that shape or influence adult life. For a child with additional needs and their families these can be multiplied, and a justifiable cause of anxieties and concerns due to the complexities and responsibilities these decisions may carry. For example, any young adult approaching adulthood at 18 has to consider educational options, which could be college courses (including where to attend college), or employment options (working full-time, part-time, apprenticeships, vocational training), and what career path they may wish to pursue. There are also decisions around housing – to remain living with parents, living with friends or others. These decisions are just as relevant to young adults with additional needs, although they carry other complexities and require additional support to make these arrangements. Many of these issues are explored in more depth in other chapters, but this chapter aims to explore and explain the arrangements for the actual decision-making and roles and responsibilities within this process. It aims to provide a practice framework for transition practitioners, and best practice examples for supporting in this area.

BACKGROUND

It needs to be recognised and acknowledged that young adults with additional needs have a right to be enabled to make choices for themselves, and to have as much control over their lives as anyone else. Historically, for people with a learning disability this was not the case, as they were routinely denied choice – for example, in long-stay hospitals, choices were made on their behalf as to even the most basic things such as what they would wear or do in any given day. For those living with families this may have been less restrictive, but nonetheless, many decisions would be made by other family members. There have been significant changes to this view, triggered by several movements such as the Civil Rights Movement, the normalisation movement and the development of the social model of disability. The movement towards personalisation, as can be seen from the previous chapter, is constructed around the tenet that people should be empowered to take choice and control over their options, and that practitioners should be in a position to provide people with the appropriate information, support and guidance needed to make well-informed decisions and choices.

DECISION-MAKING PRE-16

Prior to the age of 16 children with a disability are assumed by law to be unable to make their own decisions on issues such as care and support, or medical treatment. Decisions of this nature are generally made on their behalf by a parent, or by whoever holds 'parental responsibility', in conjunction with the involved professionals (Parker *et al.* 2013). Parental responsibility is a central tenet that runs through the Children Act 1989. Brammer (2007) states that it is defined as 'all of the rights, duties, powers, responsibilities, and authority which by law a parent of a child has in relation to the child and his property'. Usually both parents will hold parental responsibility, but unmarried fathers will need to take steps to acquire this. In some cases it may be shared – for example, if the young person is subject to a Care Order, parental responsibility would be shared with the local authority (Parker *et al.* 2013).

However, there may be some cases in which a child is considered to have the understanding and maturity to make some decisions for themselves prior to 16, as the law considers them to be 'Gillick competent'. In the Gillick case, the Court ruled that if a person under 16 had sufficient understanding, they may give consent (to treatment, in the Gillick case) in the absence of parental consent, it is not necessary to inform the parent, and the decision-making should not be determined by a judicially fixed age limit (Brammer 2007).

DECISION-MAKING POST-16

Between the ages of 16–17 it is assumed by the practitioner working with the young person that in terms of the assessment process, the young person is able to make their own decisions, unless there is evidence to suggest that they are not. If there are suggestions or evidence to support the view that they are unable to independently make decisions, the Mental Capacity Act 2005 applies.

Although this is viewed as a piece of adult legislation, it does apply from the age of 16. If a decision is required, for example, around accepting treatment or change of provision, practitioners are required to complete a mental capacity assessment, if deemed necessary, and if the young person is found to lack capacity, a decision needs to be made in their 'best interests', involving parents and other key people in their life. The role of the parent/carer is paramount – their views and wishes should not be ignored, and they should not be excluded from the decision-making that is likely to impact on them and their wider family.

This may come as a culture shock for family carers who are accustomed to making all of the decisions on behalf of their children. They often view this transfer of power to their child as extremely difficult to comprehend, particularly if their child has complex needs. The benefit of transition practitioners working with the young adult and their family from an earlier age than 18 is that they can support this shift in a positive way by preparing the family carer, identifying early on some of the issues that may require decision-making. They are best placed to support the young adult and their family carers by talking through the issues, providing information and an overview of the legislation. By providing this support and reassurance before decisions are necessary, this can often dispel some of the anxieties.

MENTAL CAPACITY ACT 2005

The Mental Capacity Act 2005 provides a statutory framework for decision-making for people over the age of 16 who are deemed to lack the capacity to make some decisions for themselves.

It provides a single definition of a lack of capacity, which was previously unclear and nebulous for practitioners, and could be subject to differing interpretations and understanding of what this meant in practice. Section 2 of the Act states that 'a person lacks capacity in relation to a matter if at the material time he is to make a decision for himself in relation to the matter because of an impairment of, or a disturbance in the functioning of, the mind or brain'.

It encompasses five key principles that are integral to practitioners working within the Act:

- *A person must be assumed to have capacity unless it is established that they lack capacity*: Historically, for practitioners working within transition, this may have applied to working with someone with a learning disability. They may have approached the situation within assessment when a decision was required that based on their diagnosis they lacked capacity to make this, although this principle ensures that this assumption must be tested, evidenced and recorded under a formal mental capacity assessment.

- *A person is not to be treated as unable to make a decision unless all practicable steps to help them to do so have been taken without success*: This may mean for practitioners undertaking assessments that alternative environ-ments, communication methods or alternative ways of providing the relevant information may be required. This is explored further later in this chapter.

- *A person is not to be treated as unable to make a decision because they have made unwise decisions*: This means for practitioners, particularly in transition, that young people cannot be assumed to lack capacity because they have previously made decisions that can be seen as unwise. Practitioners need to take into account that people often make decisions that other people see as unwise, particularly within this age group and life stage maturation, and this cannot be used to discriminate against a young person in all aspects of decision-making.

- *Any decision made under the Act, on behalf of someone who lacks capacity, must be made in their best interests*: This is explicit for practitioners to determine and evidence why this decision is made in their best interests, adhering to establishing the wishes, views and feelings of the person and consulting others who are important to the person. This could be a parent/carer, but could equally be a sibling, friend or anyone that the person views as important in their life.

- *The least restrictive options must be considered before a decision is made*: This should be seen as an overarching principle in working with vulnerable people, but is particularly important for young people in transition. This could mean, for example, if a young person's parent/ carer is unable to meet their needs and the decision is around moving that young person on to alternative provision, it should be considered whether a package of support provided at home, or day services outside of the home, may meet the young person's needs in a less restrictive manner than moving the young person on to live somewhere else.

MENTAL CAPACITY ASSESSMENT

A mental capacity assessment can only be made in relation to a specific decision at a specific time. It is important for practitioners to adhere to this and not assume that because a young person lacks capacity in one distinct area, this doesn't mean a blanket decision that covers all areas. For example, a young person may have been assessed as lacking capacity to manage a bank account, but this doesn't mean that they lack capacity to nominate someone to do this on their behalf. All decisions need to be viewed as distinct and specific, without assuming that capacity is lacked in other areas.

The assessment itself is a two-stage approach to determining capacity. The first condition that must be met is establishing that the young person has an *impairment or disturbance in the functioning of the mind or brain*. For example, a young person with a learning disability, a level of learning difficulties, an acquired brain injury, or any condition that would alter cognitive function, would qualify in this criterion. In terms of recording the assessment, practitioners should ensure that any diagnosis is recorded, along with the name of the doctor who made the diagnosis, and the date it was diagnosed, as this evidences that it has been properly established that the young person meets this first diagnostic test.

Once this has been established, there are four elements to the Section 3 test – a person is unable to make a decision for themselves if they are unable to:

- understand the relevant information

- retain the relevant information

- weigh up the information in order to make the decision

- communicate the decision.

If someone is unable to meet any one of these elements, they are deemed to lack capacity.

However, before considering the Mental Capacity Act, it should be noted that for practitioners working with young people, the first principle of the Act is that someone must be assumed to have capacity unless there is evidence to suggest that they lack capacity. Therefore the first step when working with a young person when a decision has been identified that must be made is to provide the correct information, advice and support necessary to empower the young person to make the decision for themselves. The need to provide information is enshrined in policy – the *Adult Social Care Outcomes Framework 2014 to 2015* (DH 2013b) gives measures that must be achieved, including that everybody can access support and information to help them manage care needs, but also that people know what choices are available to them locally, and what they are entitled to. The Care Bill has also made this a responsibility for local authorities once implemented, and Think Local, Act Personal have used access to information as a marker for demonstrating that services are truly personalised. Research in Practice for Adults (RIPFA) (2013) has identified that in terms of good practice, the right information, at the right time and place, and in the right way, is vital, and this has been plotted against a table of how it can be achieved.

WHICH DECISIONS?

The information required is obviously dependent on the decision that needs to be made. The decisions to be made during the transition period for a young person can be multiple, as all young people are individuals and their situations are unique, and they can also vary in contentiousness and complexity. The most common decision, however, within this age group is around their finances, whether this is in general terms around receipt of benefits, opening a bank account, how their money can be spent, and also how their direct payment or personal budget could be managed and spent.

This is particularly pertinent to young people in transition, as 16 is the age when young people become entitled to benefits and financial support in their own right, despite where they live and who they live with. The young person's finances and management of them could constitute one decision or it could be made up of a number of decisions that may require mental capacity assessments and best interest decisions to be made.

Decisions around finances are often needed in the transition to adulthood, whether this is about who manages their benefits and how, or who is best placed to manage a personal budget, or indeed, some young adults with additional needs may have a trust fund or compensation monies that require management on their behalf. Choice of accommodation is also a common but extremely complex decision that is required – where to live, whether this is supported living, residential care, to remain with family or to access local housing, and who to live with under what arrangements. This could require a number of separate decisions that carry equal weight and that need to be worked through by practitioners in partnership with the young person and their family or carers. Many of these decisions may be contentious or emotive, and need highly skilled practitioners to identify the decision and provide the relevant information, in a timely manner and in the correct format for the young person and their family to understand the decision needed and any potential risks and consequences. These decisions and this level of decision-making are not unique to transitions, however, although it needs to be recognised that this is an area that transition practitioners need to be especially skilled in, as it is a life stage that requires multiple decisions.

If it is identified, as part of an assessment for a young person with a learning disability, that a decision is required, for example, about the management of a personal budget, practitioners must take several elements into account, under the principles of the Mental Capacity Act. Therefore they must assume that the young person has capacity to make the decision as to who they want to manage this budget, whether it is independently, or whether they nominate another person. The decision that is needed and the options available need to be explored with the young person and their carer, if appropriate, as part of the assessment process. Practitioners must also have expert knowledge of what is meant by capacity, and the lack of capacity, as well as using an anti-oppressive approach that does not discriminate on the basis of age, appearance or condition (Brown 2010).

TRANSITION PRACTITIONER TIPS

- Consider what information and options would be needed to ensure the young person can make the decision themselves, and how these need to be presented in order to make an informed decision, but also to allow you to gain a good understanding of how that young person reaches a decision. For example, a young person with a learning disability may need the information to be presented in an easy read format, or use a signing system such as Makaton; a young person with a hearing impairment may need a signer; or a young person whose first language is not English may require an interpreter (Koprawska 2010).

- Individualised communication boards could also be used, as well electronic devices such as LAMPS or specialist apps for iPads, tablets or Smartphones. If appropriate, you could also use other key people in the young person's life to support the presentation of the information – for example, teaching staff could use it to form an educational activity.

- Take into account the environment and time of day that the assessment takes place, in order to provide the young person with the best possible opportunity to make the decision independently.

CASE STUDY – DANIEL

Daniel is a 17-year-old young man with a learning disability, who is approaching his eighteenth birthday and is working with a transition practitioner on an assessment of his care needs. When he was 16 he was supported by his mother to open his own bank account to receive, and manage, his own benefits. This was a very basic bank account that did not allow Daniel to go overdrawn, and by budgeting with his mother, he had a pre-agreed amount he could withdraw and spend. This has worked well for Daniel, and increased his confidence in this area of his life. Daniel had previously stated that he had a cousin and a friend he wished to employ to support his care needs as an adult, and his mother was supportive of this arrangement. The transition worker was therefore exploring the use of a personal budget for Daniel, as this would allow him to meet this outcome.

The decisions that Daniel needed to make in this situation are: did he wish to receive a personal budget, did he want to manage the budget, or did he want someone to manage it on his behalf?

To support Daniel with understanding and making these decisions, the transition worker needs to consider what additional information or support he would need to do this. This could be, for example, a written information pack about personal budgets, or it could be an easy read version, with or without symbols. It could be a Penderels independent living adviser (commissioned to provide employment support with a direct payment) or another contracted employment support provider, to explain their role in supporting Daniel to manage his personal budget and employing assistants. It could be that information is left with his mother to talk through with Daniel, in order for them to return to this in smaller chunks so that he does not become overwhelmed. The transition worker may have links with Daniel's school and ask that this may be made a topic for students to discuss more generally, as young people will often more freely discuss issues with their peers rather than professionals.

If, after providing as much additional information and support as may be necessary, there are still doubts about Daniel's capacity to manage his budget independently, the transition worker needs to begin a mental capacity assessment. As Daniel has a diagnosed learning disability, he meets the first stage of the two-staged approach as he has a cognitive impairment. The transition worker needs to discuss with Daniel and his family how, where, and when the assessment needs to take place to ensure Daniel is as comfortable and supported as possible, in order to maximise his potential for capacity at that time. For Daniel this was in his own home mid-morning, before he became hungry for his lunch, and also to have his mother with him during the assessment.

The worker then needs to consider what information needs to be presented to Daniel, and how, in order for him to understand what is being asked. Daniel's preference is for easy read information but without symbols as they make him feel like a small child rather than an adult. The transition worker had already established during working with Daniel that he preferred a 'narrative' approach, which was more like a conversation than a questioning model, as this made him feel additionally empowered in his answers rather than feeling like there was a potential for 'wrong answers'.

Daniel was able to understand the relevant information as it was presented; however, he was unable to retain the relevant information, or to use it to weigh up the relevant information, but he was able to communicate his wish to manage his personal budget. As this evidenced that Daniel did not have capacity to make this particular decision, in partnership with Daniel and his mother, the transition worker was able to reach the decision in Daniel's best interests that his mother would manage the budget on Daniel's behalf (sometimes referred to as a facilitated budget with a mother as a 'suitable person'), but with Daniel's full involvement, where he was able. Daniel will retain management over his current account, as this remains unaffected by this decision as it is time- and decision-specific, and by allowing his mother to manage the budget on his behalf, this is less restrictive than other options. There may be other assessments necessary for Daniel around other decisions, but the fact that he has lacked capacity in this instance should not pre-empt the outcomes of other decisions. Neither does it mean that he will never have capacity to manage his own budget, as he may learn these skills or be subject to certain life experiences which could mean that his understanding is increased, and he can then apply that understanding to his decision-making.

Other common decisions required during transition are often around change of accommodation, including issues such as choice of accommodation, who to live with, where to live, and how individual support needs will be met. These issues can be particularly applicable to the most vulnerable and complex of young people with disabilities whose needs may have been previously met in children's homes or specialist residential schools, who need to move on, either at their eighteenth birthday or in July of their last year in education, depending on the arrangement.

CASE STUDY – GEORGE

George is a young man with a severe learning disability and complex autism needs, who can display some physically challenging behaviour when anxious. He is mainly non-verbal, but staff at school had been working closely with a speech and language therapist who introduced the use of a specialist app on his iPad to facilitate his communication needs, and this proved successful. He was placed at a specialist autism provision as a child as his family struggled to cope with his complex needs. George has a skilled staff team that have a good awareness of his needs, but they are also skilled in assessing his risk, both to himself and others. George is approaching his transition as he is about to start his final year in education.

The transition worker had completed his adult assessment of need by working in partnership with staff at the provision, and gathering information, both from historic files and from family members, and also observations of George in his education and residential settings. As there was a clear need for George to move on from his current accommodation as they were a registered children's provision, and there was sufficient evidence that George's capacity for decision-making was impaired, a mental capacity assessment was required to establish how this need could be met.

Due to George's complex communication needs, combined with heightened anxieties around change and the risk this could pose towards staff, this needed to be carefully managed. The transition worker proceeded, in partnership with the staff that knew him well, to look at the questions that would need to be asked of George to establish his ability to make this decision. The staff team then interpreted these questions into his app, and ensured there was enough choice within his app for George to respond with his preferences, wishes and feelings. The actual assessment was then facilitated by the staff team that he knew and trusted, but observed by the transition worker. As George had previously seen the transition worker in various settings, this did not increase his anxiety significantly.

The assessment found that George did not have the capacity to choose where he wanted to live following the end of his education, but he was able to identify that he liked living with other young people, and that he enjoyed contact with his family, but also that access to a swing seat was very important to him. Working in this way provided an understanding of what was important to George and the elements that needed to be considered in his future.

It is difficult for a transition worker to provide a young person with absolutes – for example, in this case it is impossible to provide George with pictures or details of likely accommodation, whether this is residential or supported living, as it is unlikely at this stage that these 'absolutes' would have been identified, and it could be argued that by dealing in very abstract concepts, this doesn't maximise the capacity of a young person to make such an important decision. However, with the support of an IMCA, George's family and the continued support of staff, when possible placements that fit the criteria for George are identified, choices can be offered in a more meaningful way. The process of transition is a lengthy one, and it needs to be recognised that these assessments can be fluid and repeated when needed.

Both of these case studies have identified the use of alternative communication methods as a means of providing the young people with information in a way that they can better understand, which then maximises the young person's ability to make decisions, or indicate their preferences and wishes. Difficulties in communication are often accompanied by a learning disability, and research estimates that between 50 and 90 per cent of people with a learning disability have some degree of communication difficulties (Emerson and Einfield 2001). Meeting these support needs can vary from individual to individual, and is dependent on whether the difficulties are based on understanding what is being communicated (receptive difficulties), or expressing what they want to communicate (expressive difficulties), or both.

ROLE OF THE INDEPENDENT MENTAL CAPACITY ADVOCATE

Part of the role of a social worker is often acting as an advocate for the service user, giving them a voice, or supporting them to speak for themselves (Beckett 2006). However, when a service user, or in these cases a young adult, lacks capacity, there can be a need for a specialist advocate role, an IMCA, which is a recognised and required role under the Mental Capacity Act. It is a requirement of the Act that when a person lacks capacity around a specific decision which is important, for example, where to live, and they do not have family or friends to represent them in the best interests process, an IMCA must be appointed to represent them (Brown *et al.* 2008). There is a duty to appoint an IMCA for change in long-term accommodation and also serious medical treatment. There is also discretion to appoint an IMCA for reviews of care or adult protection proceedings, even if there are friends or family in place, if the involved practitioner can evidence the benefit of this. For example, a transition practitioner may feel that the young person could benefit from the services of an IMCA if the involved family has a history of not making decisions in the person's best interests, or they have consistently undermined care arrangements.

The Mental Capacity Act 2005 Code of Practice (DCA 2007) provides a summary of the IMCA's role, but it is essentially to decide how to best represent and support the person who lacks capacity in a variety of ways. They must confirm that they are being instructed by someone with the authority to do so – a transition worker would have this authority, as would a residential provision working with a young person. They must meet and interview the young person in private, if possible; if this is not possible, due to risk, this must be recorded. They may examine and have access to any relevant records about that young person, but also gather the views of the involved professionals, paid workers or any others who can provide information about the wishes, feelings, values or beliefs of the young person lacking capacity. They must also try to establish what these wishes and feelings would be if the young person did have capacity, in order to judge what their preference may be in the specific decision. They must find out what has been done to maximise the young person's capacity in this decision, and explore what alternative options there may be, and then construct a report on these findings for the authority that appointed them (in this case, the transition worker). The IMCA must act at all times in accordance with the principles of the Act while taking account of the relevant guidance in the Code.

A transition worker, working effectively with an IMCA, is key to ensuring that young people in transition are well supported and represented in the decision-making process around change of accommodation, especially the most vulnerable young people who do not have supportive family or friends to support them. If an IMCA is appointed to support a young person through a change of accommodation, they should also be requested to be part of the review of that service, as this helps to ensure that the accommodation remains suitable, meeting that young person's needs, while supporting their desired outcomes. However, a national annual review of the IMCA service showed that although the number of referrals in relation to care reviews have increased, concerns were raised that this figure remains low in comparison for referrals to accommodation decisions, and this may be suggestive that reviews are not being held consistently in line with the guidance that suggests that they should be convened three months after any move to new accommodation (Kennedy 2014).

DEPRIVATION OF LIBERTY SAFEGUARDS

An IMCA is a safeguard that is in place under the Mental Capacity Act 2005, but there is also a specific role for IMCAs to support people who may be subject to Deprivation of Liberty Safeguards (DoLS), which were introduced in 2009. This legislation aims to protect those who can't make decisions about treatment or care, who need to be cared for in a restrictive manner, and this must be used if people are having their liberty taken away in order to receive this treatment or care that is in their best interests and protects them from harm. For young adults in transition this needs to be considered if they are living in a care home or hospital which has locked doors, which uses restraints to protect the young person or paid carers, or in which they are subject to regular monitoring. Any of these elements alone may not be counted as a deprivation of their liberty, but the presence of any of these measures needs careful consideration.

These safeguards affect people living in care homes or hospitals over the age of 18 who suffer from a mental disorder, lack the capacity to give consent to their care arrangements, for whom a DoLS is believed to be necessary and proportionate, and in their best interests to protect them from harm, and for whom detention under the Mental Health Act 1983 is not appropriate.

If a transition worker, when working with a young person, feels that they may be being deprived of their liberty in a care home or hospital, they must work with the registered manager of the home, or the managing authority, who will refer to the local authority (or supervisor body) for authorisation. Following this will be a six-stage assessment by a minimum of two assessors to establish if a deprivation of liberty is occurring, or going to occur, and if so, whether it is in the person's best interests, whether it is necessary to prevent harm, and if it is proportionate. More information on this process can be accessed via the DoLS Code of Practice (Ministry of Justice 2008).

CASE STUDY – AARON

Aaron is 18 years old and has an acquired brain injury. He has been accommodated as a child in a specialist educational provision due to his mother's neglect and eventual abandonment. Aaron has always stated his wish to return home to his family at 18, and his behaviour can become challenging towards staff or professionals if alternative arrangements are suggested. The transition worker is planning to move Aaron to a specialist residential provision, close to where he lives now, that specialises in working with brain injuries. A mental capacity assessment has been completed which found that Aaron lacked capacity about his choice of accommodation, and an IMCA has been appointed to represent Aaron as his family have disengaged and were unwilling to be consulted.

A support plan has been developed which gives Aaron as much choice and control over his arrangements as possible, but the transition worker feels that the restrictions to prevent Aaron from leaving the residential provision, as well as the intense levels of monitoring to ensure his safety, are amounting to a deprivation of his liberty. A request for a standard authorisation is made from the home manager and a best interests assessor is appointed. They feel that the proposed support plan is necessary, proportionate, and is in Aaron's best interests, and recommend a standard authorisation for six months in the first instance.

It is important to note that at the time of writing DoLS does not apply to people lacking capacity residing in group homes or supported living accommodation. With the onus on local authorities to ensure that residential care is not the preferred option for young people, and that supported living is seen as a preferable alternative, this could be viewed as a barrier to ensuring that young people are not being deprived of their liberty, and an important consideration for transition workers. However, under the recent case law established by Cheshire West and Chester Council ruling, this could potentially widen the DoLS environments to include supported living, day care and the young person's family home.

COURT OF PROTECTION

The Court of Protection may be necessary to access when working with a young person who lacks capacity. It deals with all issues concerning people who lack capacity, including, but not restricted to, orders in respect of their property and affairs, personal welfare, making medical decisions, deprivation of liberties, determining where they should live, contact arrangements, and consent or refusal of serious medical treatment. For example, a suitable person may make an application to the Court of Protection, to be appointed as a deputy to manage property and affairs, or to sign a tenancy agreement. Tenancy agreements are becoming increasingly more common to apply for within this transition group of young people, as supported living set-ups, in which the person has their own tenancy, are seen as a preferred option. The Court of Protection can also be used when there has been a dispute that cannot be resolved.

CONCLUSION

This chapter has aimed to explore some of the decisions that are relevant to young people with additional needs in their transition to adulthood, and to examine the frameworks, and specific roles and responsibilities that are in place to support positive decision-making for young people and their families. Many of these decisions can be seen as tiered, with most simple decisions being made by the young person with support, to more complex decisions – particularly around accommodation and finances – requiring the support of a professional completing a formal assessment. The Mental Capacity Act can be seen as a powerful tool for practitioners to support and empower young people to make decisions as independently as possible. Transition workers need to be especially knowledgeable and skilled in utilising the Act to empower young people to maximise their capacity to make some of these decisions. Working with family and carers is also key to decision-making, and indeed required under the Mental Capacity Act when implementing Best Interests. Practitioners need to feel confident in recognising how to engage family and carers to work in partnership when a best interests decision is required. There may be requirements to use an IMCA where necessary for these decisions, but there are also situations when it is good practice to involve an IMCA and practitioners need to feel confident in recognising and referring when this is required. There may be situations when DoLs needs to be considered, specifically when working with young people that lack capacity who may be placed in a children's residential provision.

The capacity of young people is key when assessing and supporting them, and practitioners must feel empowered to work within this framework effectively, to allow the young person the legal protection the Act provides them with to make their own decisions, or to have them made on their behalf, with their best interests at the heart of them.

9

TRANSITIONS AND FAMILY CARERS

INTRODUCTION

A carer can be anyone who cares, unpaid, for a family member, spouse, or friend, who, for whatever reason – health, disability (both physical), learning disability or mental health, or addiction – would not be able to manage without their support. This should not be confused or equated with people who care as a paid role, as a care worker, home care assistant or anyone paid for their support via a direct payment.

Carers can be from any culture, any age, class, gender and any background. Most carers don't actively choose to become carers – they are mothers, fathers, spouses, adult children whose loved ones are in a situation that requires additional support and assistance not met by formal means. Many carers combine caring responsibilities with paid work or other roles.

Family carers seems to be a distinct term referring specifically to someone who cares for an individual with a learning disability, usually a child, who continues to need care into adulthood.

CARERS ACROSS THE UK

- There are almost seven million carers in the UK – that is one in ten people. This is rising.

- Every year in the UK, over 2.3 million adults become carers and over 2.3 million adults stop being carers. Three in five people will be carers at some point in their lives in the UK.

- Out of the UK's carers, 42% of carers are men and 58% are women.

- The economic value of the contribution made by carers in the UK is £119bn per year.

- Over the next 30 years, the number of carers will increase by 3.4 million (around 60%).

- Up to 1.5 million people in the UK care for someone with a mental health problem.

- At the very least, nearly 1.5 million adults in the UK are affected by a relative's drug use.

- 14% of carers (approx. 840,000) care for people with learning disabilities including autistic-spectrum conditions.

(Carers Trust 2012)

The gender split among carers challenges the myth that carers are typically female. The greatest burden of care nationally falls to women aged 50–64, but for the over-65s, the proportion of male carers then exceeds female carers. The authors of the ONS report (ONS 2013) suggest that this could be because women are more likely than men to leave work at an earlier age to provide unpaid care for family members, boosting their numbers in the 50–64 age bracket (NHS UK 2014).

YOUNG CARERS

- 13,000 of the UK's young carers care for over 50 hours a week.

- Following a survey in 2010, the BBC estimated that there are 700,000 young carers in the UK.

- Young adult carers aged between 16 and 18 years are twice as likely to be not in education, employment, or training (NEET).

- In total there are 290,369 carers in the UK who are aged 16–24.

(Carers Trust 2012)

A young carer may not recognise that they are a young carer. Their perception may be that they are just helping with a brother or sister, or just helping a parent. It is good practice for transition practitioners to explore who does what within the household, for instance, what does a typical day look like? These types of questions help in identifying who is supporting who, as it can be difficult to unpick if the young carer's role is not identified by the young person, or the main carer – families may view it as just playing an active part in the family. Most local authorities have specific services in place to support young carers, and the practitioner can refer on to these if it is correctly identified.

A study conducted by Manchester Carers Forum, in conjunction with Loughborough University's Young Carers Research Group (YCRG), used in-depth interviews and psychological measures among 50 young carers living in Manchester (Abraham and Aldridge 2010). It highlighted that the number of young carers were often under-estimated, and also that a young carer's role had a significant negative impact on their health and psychological wellbeing, limiting their life chances. Similarly, a Children's Society report (Children's Society 2013)found that children acting as unpaid carers tended to underperform at school, which could adversely affect their opportunities later in life.

Transition practitioners need to be aware of these issues, and proactive in identifying young people with caring responsibilities.

OLDER CARERS

- In England and Wales, just under one million (950,000) people over 65 are carers.

- 65% of older carers (aged 60–94) have long-term health problems or a disability themselves.

- A four year study of 392 carers and 427 non-carers aged 66–92 found that carers who were reporting feelings of strain had a 63% higher likelihood of death in that period than non-carers or carers not reporting strain.

(Carers Trust 2012)

As mentioned, the share of unpaid care falls most heavily on people in the 50–64 age bracket – 24 per cent of women and 17 per cent of men of this age group provide one or more hours of unpaid care a week. Within transition, care is typically provided by parents who are unlikely to be older carers. However, a significant number of young people may be cared for by a grandparent. Transition practitioners need to be aware of the extra support needs of this group of carers, to ensure that their individual needs are met and that they receive the support so that their health and wellbeing remains paramount, as this is key to sustaining the young person they are caring for. For example, their need for residential respite provision for the young person could be vital in ensuring they have sufficient breaks from the caring role, to maintain their health. Many local authorities also offer additional services to carers over 65 in terms of dedicated carer support workers who are able to provide long-term outreach support.

EMPLOYMENT

- There are 4.27 million carers of working age living in the UK; 2.44 million (57%) of these are women and 1.83 million (43%) are men.

- The employment rate for carers is at 67% (72% of men and 62% of women); over half of those who are not working say they want to do so.

- £5.3bn has been wiped from the economy in lost earnings due to people who've dropped out of the workforce to take on caring responsibilities.

- One in five carers gives up employment to care.

(Carers Trust 2012)

If transition practitioners identify within the assessment process that a carer is caring in conjunction with paid work, it is worth checking out with them how they manage this, as this could put a significant strain on both roles. In order to support them to maintain these roles, practitioners need to be knowledgeable about the rights of a carer in employment.

The right to request flexible working has now been extended to cover all employees with 26 weeks' service or more. The request can cover changing hours, times or places of work, and can be worked in a variety of different ways:

- *Flexi-time*: employees may be required to work within set times but outside of these 'core hours' have some flexibility in how they work their hours.

- *Homeworking or teleworking*: teleworking is where employees spend part or all of their working week away from the workplace. Homeworking is just one of the types of teleworking.

- *Job sharing*: usually two employees share the work normally done by one person.

- *Part-time working*: employees might work shorter days or fewer days in a week.

- *Term-time working*: employees don't work during school holidays and either take paid or unpaid leave or their salary is calculated pro-rata over the whole year.

- *Shift-swapping or self-rostering*: employees agree shifts among themselves and negotiate with colleagues when they need time off with the process being overseen by managers.

- *Compressed hours*: employees work their total hours over fewer working days e.g. a ten day fortnight is compressed into a nine day fortnight.

(Carers UK 2014)

It may be that the options open to the carer's employers could be limited, due to the specific nature of their work, and they would therefore be unable to consider any of these options; however, this is worth a discussion with the carer.

FINANCE

- In an online survey of 800 carers completed by the Princess Royal Trust for Carers in July 2010 53% have borrowed money as a result of their caring role – 61% have borrowed from a friend or relative and 41% have used overdrafts.

- Out of the carers surveyed, 35% of carers had missed out on state benefits because they didn't realise they could claim them.

(Carers Trust 2012)

Carers UK say the main carer's benefit, Carer's Allowance, is worth just £1.71 an hour. As a result, 44 per cent of carers say they are now in debt, and nearly half (45%) report they have had to cut back on essentials such as food and heating.

The controversial 'Bedroom Tax' has cut support for an approximate 40,000 carers by an average of £700 a year, while changes in Council Tax Benefit have hit 240,000 carers.

Transition practitioners need to approach this sensitively, as families may be reluctant to discuss such debt with a social worker. In these circumstances, if debt is disclosed, it is sensible to signpost to another organisation better placed to provide support with this. There could be a potential conflict of interest if transition practitioners feel that the care of the young person is being compromised by wider issues of financial difficulties

LEGISLATIVE BACKGROUND

Carer's assessments were first mentioned in the Carers (Recognition and Services) Act 1995. This stated that carers can ask for an assessment of their own needs when the person they are caring for is having an assessment, or re-assessment, of their needs. Two later Acts have superseded this, but the 1995 Act is the only one that does not restrict carer's assessments according to age, meaning that young carers can have an assessment under this piece of legislation.

The Carers and Disabled Children Act 2000 was promised in the carer's strategy, *Caring about Carers* (DH 1999), and made some important changes to assessment and services for carers. This Act gives carers the right to ask for an assessment of their own needs to help them to continue to care, irrespective of whether the person they are caring for has had or is having their own needs assessment. The assessment is available to any carer who provides or is intending to provide regular and substantial care. The Carers and Disabled Children Act 2000 also allows, for the first time, local authorities to provide services directly to carers, although this is a local authority 'power' as opposed to a 'duty'. And if the local authority provides a carer's service, they are able to charge for that service – although many choose not to charge for services provided directly to carers.

The Carers (Equal Opportunities) Act 2004 is the most recent legislation, and was implemented in April 2005. It changes the previous Act in a few important ways. First, it places a duty on local authorities to inform carers of their right to an assessment. Second, when the assessment is carried out, its purpose is not only to help the carer to continue to care, but it should also include a discussion on outcomes they wish to achieve, for example, around employment, education and leisure. Third, carers and their needs have previously only been a duty for social service departments, but under this Act, local authorities can ask other public bodies, including local health organisations, to provide services to carers (Carers Trust n.d.).

ASSESSMENTS UNDER THE CHILDREN ACT
Parents and carers of a child with disabilities may be assessed under the Children Act as local authorities have a duty to assess a child with a disability as a 'child in need'. Depending on the circumstances of the child, an initial assessment will be carried out, which will involve information-gathering from the child and other involved agencies, and also direct information-gathering from the main carer and other key family members. This could be followed by a core assessment, depending on the circumstances, which is a more in-depth assessment, and various other agencies may be contacted to complete specialist assessments or reports. Services may then be provided to meet the needs of the child as identified within this assessment. This should

also support the carer as providing specialist services to the child reduces pressure on the main carer.

Some children with additional needs may be assessed via the Common Assessment Framework (CAF). This doesn't replace the assessment framework for a child in need, but it can prove to be effective for a child with a disability to identify unmet needs, both for the child and for the family carer. It looks at needs holistically rather than needs that may be met by one agency, and that are carried out in a range of settings by a potential range of professionals such as teachers or health and social care professionals.

If a carer doesn't feel that their needs have been fully recognised, as part of the assessment under the Children Act they can request a carer's assessment in their own right. It should be noted, however, that any services that may ordinarily be provided following a carer's assessment, for a young person over the age of 18, may not be provided to the carer of a young person under 18.

CARER'S ASSESSMENTS POST-18

As can be seen, carers have a legal right to an assessment of their needs when the person they care for reaches 18. This is an opportunity to discuss with a social worker or other relevant professional (in some authorities, this function is done by another organisation such as Carers UK) to identify what support is needed to sustain the caring role, and also to support the carer to achieve the outcomes that are identified. It should be seen as separate and distinct to the support provided to the person who is cared for, and should take into account the impact of caring on the everyday life of the carer, including their health and wellbeing and the impact on family life as a whole. A carer's assessment can also be requested when the person cared for is not in receipt of services in their own right, or if they have refused an assessment.

A carer is eligible for a separate assessment when:

- they are providing regular and substantial care

- the carer is over 16

- the individual being cared for is over 18 and would be eligible for community care services

- it is part of a planned discharge from hospital

- the person cared for is someone with a mental health problem who is subject to a CPA

- the assessment of the child under the Children Act does not take full account of the needs of the carer, for a parent/care of a child with disabilities under the age of 18.

POTENTIAL SERVICES THAT MAY SUSTAIN THE CARING ROLE

There are various services that may be available to support a carer to take a break from their caring role:

- residential respite, where the person being cared for stays somewhere else, such as a residential home or a nursing home, or an adapted holiday site

- domiciliary care, where there is support in the family home, either during the day or overnight, to enable the parent/carer to have some time to themselves

- activities for the young person such as day services, community support or school may also provide the carer with a break.

Most local authorities can also provide the carer with a direct payment or personal budget in lieu of the provision of these services. Skilled transition workers can work directly with the carer in order to plan something that may meet their needs more creatively or that are bespoke to the family. By working with both the young person and the carer over a longer period of time, this ensures that post-18 the support that is provided for the young person will build in opportunities for the carer to have a break, as it is recognised that sustaining the caring role is key to maintaining the young person within the family, if that is what the long-term plan is.

CASE STUDY – MARTIN

Martin is 17 years old and has a diagnosis of autism and learning disability, and can exhibit some challenging behaviour when anxious. He has also been diagnosed with mental health difficulties, with episodes of paranoia and high anxiety. Martin lives with his parents, and a younger sibling, and is supported mainly by his mother, Pam. Pam was previously employed as a project manager, and had given up this role to maintain Martin at home. Martin's school became increasingly unable to manage Martin within the educational environment, due to his behaviour, particularly during his episodes. This meant that Pam was no longer able to depend on Martin attending school; as a result, she was providing increased levels of care, with little chance of a break from her caring role. Martin also became increasingly dependent on Pam, and would often refuse to leave the house without her, or leave the family home at all.

The transition practitioner recognised the importance of Pam's role as this was key to maintaining Martin at home, and this is what the family wanted for Martin. As Martin was reluctant to leave the home, support services were introduced to Martin and Pam, to provide activities within the home. These were initially short sessions to enable Martin to get used to seeing the workers within the home, and for the workers to build up a picture of Martin and his likes and dislikes. This allowed them to plan bespoke activities initially within the home, but to then escalate this to activities in the community.

This relieved Pam of her caring role for very short periods of time. When Martin reached 18, Pam was then eligible for a carer's assessment to look at specific services that could be used to relieve her stress. This allowed Pam the space and time to tell 'her story', and support to identify her own solutions. Pam is passionately committed to Martin and would not consider any options which would cause him distress, such as a residential option. During the course of the assessment Pam identified that when she was previously employed she would often have Reiki sessions as a way of decreasing her stress, but was not now able to do so due to both the lack of time and also that she was not in a financial position to afford it, as she was not in employment.

The transition worker recognised that accessing Reiki would meet the carer's outcome of stress relief, and also provide her with a break from caring. She applied for a carer's direct payment of £250 from the local authority, and then set about to identify a Reiki practitioner who would visit Pam at home. This was enough to provide Pam with regular fortnightly sessions which could be arranged for when Martin was being supported within the family home. As Martin was also receiving regular support within the home, this provided Pam with consistent breaks which allowed her to complete tasks in the home, and was also a break to recharge her batteries and give her some time to herself.

CARER'S ALLOWANCE

Finances can often be a huge issue for carers, who may have given up employment to care for a friend, family member, or spouse. The caring role can often prevent the carer from working as they may not be able to work regular hours, or commit to shifts either full-time or part-time due to the demands of the person they care for.

Carer's Allowance is the main benefit that carers are eligible for, but this is dependent on providing care for more than 35 hours a week. It is paid at £61.35 a week (2014–15 rates). The amount of benefit is usually increased each April. Although this is a taxable benefit, carers only have to pay tax if they have other sources of taxable income such as paid earnings, but the benefit alone is below the threshold for paying tax. It is not means-tested, and not dependent on the carer's National Insurance. (A benefits table is included in Appendix 1 for reference.)

In order to be eligible for Carer's Allowance the following conditions must be met (Carers UK n.d.):

- The young person being cared for must be in receipt of a disability-related benefit (such as Disability Living Allowance, DLA).

- The care provided must be over 35 hours a week.

- The carer must be aged over 16.

- The carer cannot be in full-time education.

- The carer must be a UK resident.

Within transition it is important that practitioners are aware of what benefits the young person and their family may be eligible to claim. This can enable practitioners to ensure that the funds available to the family are maximised, because if the family are living below the poverty line, this can have long-term consequences on their health and wellbeing. It also enables practitioners to support the plan creatively, using the resources that are available. For example, if a personal budget had been awarded, and transport was an integral part of the support provided, then it maximises the budget if the young person was using the transport element of their DLA to meet this element of support, rather than using their personal budget to access transport (see the benefits table in Appendix 1). This gets the best value of the support needed in terms of hours or additional support.

It is not the role of practitioners to support the family to apply for any benefits they may be eligible for, but they must be able to effectively signpost the young person and their family to other agencies that can fulfil this task. It is worthwhile therefore to become familiar with voluntary agencies within the local area that can help with those tasks that are outside of the practitioner's role.

ISSUES SPECIFIC TO CARERS AT TRANSITION

A project was carried out in 2004 by the Norah Fry Research Centre, in conjunction with North Somerset People First and the Home Farm Trust, to explore issues relating to the needs of young people, their supporters and their families at transition (SCIE 2004). The report looked at what information was needed for transition, as well as evaluating and reviewing the available literature, information packs and materials available to support transition. The project was carried out using focus group interviews, a review of the literature and an evaluation of the materials by young people and their families. For the purposes of this chapter I concentrate on the identified carer's issues.

During the introduction phase of the interviews parents/carers were asked 'What is transition?' The main answers were fairly accurate, as in being about their young person becoming an adult, but it also generated emotive responses such as 'scary' and 'frightening', with specific concerns around a lack of appropriate services and of transition planning. A quote from a parent likened it to 'crystal ball gazing'.

The parents/carers highlighted awareness of a lack of appropriate services, and that services their young people could access as teenagers would be stopped. One parent noted that, 'You lose advocacy, youth centres etc. at 25.' They recognised, however, that it was a time when the young person was beginning to take charge of their life, but this was tempered with concerns about taking on some of the responsibilities that inevitably follow. There were specific concerns around their vulnerability within the community due to exhibiting behaviour that was not age-appropriate, and conversely, when their appearance could make them appear more able than they were. They noted that this could also impact on the young people's self-esteem: that it could cause 'increasing awareness of the differences between themselves and others. The parents commented that the school provided a key resource at transition, as did the local advocacy groups. This tied in with concerns that services were lost when the young people reached key ages.

A theme of the interviews undertaken by the project asked, 'What information do parents want?' This demonstrated to the project facilitators that parents were often unaware that transition was more than just leaving school, underpinned by a common assumption that their children would attend college as a taken-for-granted next step. Due to this, their information needs were directly related to their lack of understanding of the transition process. In the cases of parents of older children, they had experienced little transition planning, whereas those with younger adults were concerned about the role that they would play in the process.

The project found that the parents' information needs fell into three areas:

- *Process*: what were their rights and entitlements, and what procedures existed at national and local level? Most of the parents had little awareness of the formal process of transition, and had specific questions around, 'What do I need to know as a parent?' 'Where do I start?' 'What is available next?' 'What are we eligible for?' The interviews with those supporting reinforced this, as in their experience parents typically asked questions such as, 'Will I be included in decision-making?' 'Who can I talk to about my fears?' 'Who can I voice my opinions to?' 'Will they keep me informed?'

- *Support*: what support was available for the transition period? Parents specifically wanted to know who would support their young person in different contexts such as work, home and social life. There were also questions around local post-18 respite provision. Those supporting felt that parents needed continuous support from a single point of contact who would provide feedback and information. Parents also felt that they needed support and advice in their own right regarding the transition process and the inevitable changes that would occur within their family.

- *Information*: what was available regarding the changes and choices locally? The responses that this generated matched what the young people themselves had stated during their interviews:

  - *Work*: parents wanted information about local work opportunities, work experience and work placements, and the support that was available to their young people in these contexts.

  - *College*: parents wanted specific guidance as to appropriate courses and options and advice about residential college.

  - *Day services*: these were mentioned in terms of what young people may do following college, but did not feature prominently during the interviews.

  - *Money*: parents wanted 'easy to understand' information on benefits and entitlements post-18.

  - *Safety*: parents wanted to know how they could ensure that their young person was safe.

  - *Housing*: parents wanted information on the housing options available.

  - *Sex and relationships*: parents wanted support to help them approach this, and acknowledged that they found this difficult. They had specific concerns about the young person being taken advantage of due to their vulnerability. They also wanted to know about how much information to provide, and how to provide it. One parent said, 'Do you leave them alone with their girlfriend?' while another said, 'How personal do you get about sex without giving too much away?'

  - *Having fun*: the parents wanted information on local social events and leisure activities.

  - *Health issues*: this discussion was mainly around medical appointments and specific conditions rather than healthy living issues.

TRANSITION PRACTITIONER TIPS

- Carers need to have a full understanding of the transition process – rather than seeing it as a natural progression from school to college, they need to be aware that the decisions can be bigger than this, and that other options are available. To meet this need, you can begin to share this information with a young person from the age of 16, and this can then be discussed and thought about from an earlier stage. It is a fine line between informing carers and overwhelming already anxious parents about a process that is two to three years in the planning. Some carers will require a more measured approach, with information provided in small chunks, over a longer period of time, whereas others will prefer the bigger picture from the outset, as this will allow them to go off and research their options.

- As mentioned in Chapter 4, drop-in sessions at local specialist schools can provide a forum for information and signposting. This could potentially support carers whose children are younger than 16 to start gathering this information earlier, if that is needed.

- Most local authorities have websites that advertise and signpost local support services – depending on the quality of these websites, they can be an invaluable resource to gather information. Carers can be directed towards these, but you could also arrange this information in terms of specific local areas in order to disseminate this to specific schools or catchment areas.

CASE STUDY – NORTHAMPTONSHIRE COUNTY COUNCIL WEBSITE AND NEWSLETTER

Northamptonshire County Council have developed a website in conjunction with young people that provides information about the different teams that the young person may work with, services that they may access, eligibility for services, the assessment process and other relevant information. This is produced in easy read format, using symbols and pictures. It also includes links to PDF documents for parents/carers, and others where the information is more in-depth. This effectively provides an information service that is accessible to both the young people and carers, that meets the needs identified within the Norah Fry project (SCIE 2004). In addition to this they also produce a e-newsletter, also in easy read, which is distributed electronically as well as being accessible from their website. This includes events, interviews and case studies, which also supports the parents'/carers' need for information, as well as providing examples of how support can be delivered. They have used social media effectively by linking this with Facebook and Twitter, and also Pinterest, by developing boards of photographs from direct work with young people, events and forums.

TRANSITION PRACTITIONER TIPS

- Organise and gather factsheets regarding the themes identified in the project. Speech and language therapists will often have resources within these themes that are in easy read or plain English format that can be used or amended to address the needs of carers with a young person in transition.

- Ensure that for a young person under 18 the carer feels that their needs were fully considered during the children's assessment, and that their needs have been met via services in place for the young person. If not, a carer's assessment should be offered instead.

- Prior to the young person turning 18, the carer's assessment should be discussed and offered, with sufficient time in between for the carer to think about what they want discussed during this time, and also that the environment can be considered, as this should be done in a space that is separate from the person they provide care for – otherwise this could compromise the purpose of the assessment.

- If there is conflict between you and the carer, for whatever reason, it is good practice to consider whether you are, in fact, best placed to carry out a carer's assessment. This could be passed to a different worker, or a dedicated carer support worker, to avoid any conflict of interest during the transition. The young person needs to remain central to the transition process, and if there is conflict, this could jeopardise this support.

As highlighted during the interviews for the project, the main need that the carers identified was that of information. This needs to be provided in a timely manner in a way that is easy to understand, and can be done in a multitude of ways, whether face-to-face, printed or web-based information. Time spent putting together resources is time well spent, as once this information is gathered and stored, it can be provided over and over again. It is the skill of transition workers to ensure that this is done in the best way possible for the specific family carer, whether this is one approach or a combination of approaches.

RESOURCE

SCIE (Social Care Institute for Excellence) (2004) *The Road Ahead – Literature Review.* London and Bristol: Social Care Institute for Excellence and Norah Fry Research Centre. Available at www.scie.org.uk/publications/tra/literature/index.asp.

10

CONCLUSION

This book has shown how to achieve successful transitions for young people with disabilities, through discussion of the context of the work, the legislative overview, and practical considerations of this complex area. We have done this by theming the issues that are relevant, and using case studies to underpin certain points or issues of dilemma. The key points of these have now been themed below into age-appropriate sections for ease of reference.

TASKS FOR 14- TO 16-YEAR-OLDS
WORKING WITH CHILDREN WITH DISABILITIES TEAMS

- Regular quarterly meetings between transition workers/teams and Children with Disabilities Teams can help to improve communication and develop an understanding about the young people entering transition, what their circumstances, needs and current services are. This kind of discussion will also help to identify early on those people who are unlikely to meet adult eligibility criteria, and will allow for prompt signposting to other services.

- Provide easy read written guidance around eligibility to young people while they are still in children's services. This could be within an information pack, accessible on websites or given to young people at their 14+ review.

- Drop-in/surgery sessions at schools can be a useful way of identifying young people in the education system who may not be known to children's services, but who are likely to require support when they leave school.

DEVELOP A TRACKING SYSTEM

- A record/spreadsheet of information collected about all of the young people identified above will help in keeping track of who will require an assessment and who is in need of support. An accurate recording and monitoring system is essential to ensure that you can plan your work, pass on information to other workers, and provide accurate financial forecasts to commissioners and budget holders.

EHC PLANS

- Investigate what training or information sessions there are in your local authority around EHC plans.

- Get involved in EHC pilots if there is time, or consider ways you can input into working groups for the EHC plans.

WORK EFFECTIVELY WITH SCHOOLS

- *Connect with school*: ideally it would be good to have a link school with which you work, where you can build relationships with teaching staff, and establish what role the school will play.

- *Ask schools*: although it isn't advisable to tell schools how to do their jobs, gently reminding them of the benefits of preparing for transition reviews in advance is a good idea. Look at examples in other authorities, and suggest that schools continue to adapt these.

- *Encourage person-centred planning*: encourage young people to investigate post-school options.

- *Consider resources*: look at resources that can help gather student views – the Transition Pathway Big Picture could easily be adapted and used by schools in their timetable, and one-page profiles may help young people to think about what's important to them.

- *What can you do?*: The pressures and workloads of transition workers can be heavy and it may be hard to invest time. Look at ways you can gain the views of the young people prior to review. Could you facilitate a group where they can discuss their views?

- *Provide information*: is there accessible information for young people and families about post-school options? Is there a resource file kept in your office, or a website that young people and carers can access? Most young people want advice and guidance, and particularly in early planning, just pointing them in the right direction to access information may assist in managing their anxieties.

SEX AND RELATIONSHIPS

- Find out what resources there are locally to support young people in exploring issues around sex. Could psychology or community nurses support with sex education?

- Consider what social opportunities are available for young people to meet others such as the organisation, Stars in the Sky.

- Where appropriate, ask young people their views around sex and relationships away from family, as they may be uncomfortable discussing this in front of them.

- Identify potential risks using risk assessments and the Mental Capacity Act to support your decision-making.

TASKS FOR 17- TO 18-YEAR-OLDS
ELIGIBILITY

- The opportunity to meet with young people and screen them against eligibility criteria before their eighteenth birthday is useful. Speak with head teachers, Connexions PAs etc. to identify any young people who do not access support from children's services currently, but are likely to require support as they reach 18 or leave school.

YOUNG PEOPLE SUBJECT TO CHILD PROTECTION PLANS

- Identify why the young person is subject to a child protection plan and what the risks/potential safeguarding issues are as they enter adulthood.

- Consider early on if the young person has capacity, and how this may impact on managing safeguarding issues as they enter adulthood.

- Does the child and family have legal representation?

- What are the family and young person's expectations of what will happen at 18?

- Discuss with the adult protection team/leads and adult legal services any potential safeguarding issues, and seek direction from them.

FURTHER EDUCATION

- Find out about courses offered in your Local Offer and who is responsible in your area for making applications to the EFA. It's a good idea to make professional relationships with these representatives, whether Connexions workers or other local authority agents.

- Ask the agents what the process is for applying to residential colleges – what are their processes for making decisions, and when is a decision likely to be confirmed? Transition planning will often depend on where the young person is going for education, and if decisions about residential college are not made early enough, this will have an impact on the plan that can be put in place locally at such short notice.

HEALTH AND CONTINUING HEALTHCARE

- Familiarise yourself with the NHS CHC checklist, and consider who may be appropriate to complete these for the young people you work with. There may be a school or community nurse involved who could assist you in completing this.

- Find out how you refer for CHC assessments. Is there a dedicated CHC nurse? Do you refer to Community Learning Disabilities

Teams? Find out who is responsible for undertaking CHC assessments for people with physical disabilities.

- Meet with your local CHC team and ask them about developing a pathway/process for young people to be assessed prior to turning 18, as stated in CHC guidance.

- Ask for written information about the CHC assessment process and policy in order for you to give this to the young people and families when you meet.

FAMILY CARERS

- Carers need to have a full understanding of the transition process – rather than seeing it as a natural progression from school to college, they need to be aware that the decisions can be bigger than this, and that other options are available. To meet this need, a transition worker working with the young person from the age of 16 can begin to share this information, and this can then be discussed and thought about from an earlier stage. It is a fine line between informing carers and overwhelming already anxious parents about a process that is two to three years in the planning, however. Some carers will require a more measured approach with information provided in small chunks, over a long period of time, whereas others will prefer the bigger picture from the outset, as this will allow them to go off and research options.

- Most local authorities have websites that advertise and signpost local support services – depending on the quality of these websites, these can be an invaluable resource to gather information. Carers can be directed towards these, but you could also arrange this information in terms of specific local areas in order to disseminate this to specific schools or catchment areas.

- You could organise and gather factsheets regarding the themes identified in the project. Speech and language therapists will often have resources within these themes that are in easy read or plain English format that can be used or amended to address the needs of carers with a young person in transition.

- Ensure that for a young person under 18 the carer feels that their needs were fully considered during the children's assessment, and that their needs have been met via the services in place for the young person. If not, a Carer's Assessment should be offered instead.

- Prior to the young person turning 18, the Carer's Assessment should be discussed and offered, with sufficient time in between for the carer to think about what they want discussed during this time; the environment should also be considered, as the assessment should be done in a space that is separate from the person they provide care for – otherwise this could compromise the purpose of the assessment.

- If there is conflict between yourself and the carer, for whatever reason, it is good practice to consider whether you are, in fact, best placed to carry out a Carer's Assessment. It could be passed to a different worker, or a dedicated carer support worker, to avoid any conflict of interest during the transition. The young person needs to remain central to the transition process, and if there is conflict, this could jeopardise this support.

MENTAL CAPACITY

- Consider what information and options would be needed to ensure the young person is able to make the decision themselves, and how these need to be presented in order for the young person to make an informed decision, and also to allow you to gain a good understanding of how that young person reaches a decision. Individualised communication boards could also be used, as well as electronic devices such as LAMPS or specialist apps for iPads, tablets or Smartphones. If appropriate, you could also use other key people in the young person's life to support the presentation of the information – for example, teaching staff could use it to form an educational activity.

- Take into account the environment and time of day that it takes place, in order to provide the young person with the best possible opportunity to make the decision independently.

TASKS 18+

RESIDENTIAL/LOCAL COLLEGE

- Ensure that families and young people are aware of the options on offer.

- Ensure that a learning disability assessment is accessed at as early a stage as possible to allow time for any decisions to be challenged, particularly if residential college is the young person's preferred option.

- Ensure that the options are in line with the young person's wishes and interests, and use any skills previously learned.

UNIVERSITY APPLICATIONS

- When an institution has been chosen, make contact with their disability adviser (with the young person's consent) to look at the practical issues early on, such as accommodation, travel between campus, accommodation, and the canteen. This will then help overcome any potential barriers early on in the process.

- Ensure that a DSA assessment has been requested by the young person or their family in good time.

- Ensure that assessment for a personal budget is completed and a budget agreed to provide the maximum opportunity for support planning, as there are many variables inherent in a move to a university, including the recruitment of staff (potentially outside of the local area), allocation of accommodation, and provision of a lecture timetable.

- If there are adjustments or equipment needed for the accommodation, a referral is needed for the occupational therapist – this can be made by the social worker, the young person or the university – but ensure that in discussions, the responsibility for this task is allocated and completed to ensure this does not hold up a move.

- Think about contingencies – if they do not get the grades for their preferred choice of university, what happens then?

EMPLOYMENT

- Support the young person with the application process, or signpost them to the correct source of support. The application process can feel overwhelming to a young person who is attempting to find employment.

- Ensure that the employer is aware of their responsibilities in supporting the young person.

- Ensure regular reviews with the employer, job coach and the young person as this will flag up any potential problems, and allow time for resolving these before they become a barrier. This will also allow targets to be set, and prevent drift.

- Provide regular communication with the young person to ensure the role is meeting their needs and expectations, without the pressure of divulging issues in front of their employer.

SOCIAL ENTERPRISES

- Find out what social enterprises exist in the local area. Is there a dedicated person or service that provides a list of them?

- Are they able to meet the physical needs of the young person, or will they require a support worker to accompany them?

- How will the young person be paid for their work?

- Will it enable the young person to develop existing skills? Is it an area that they are interested in? If it isn't, will this be a sustainable option for the young person?

VOLUNTEERING

- Clarify what hours are being offered and the employer's expectation of the young person.

- Is there sufficient support for the young person there, or will additional support be required?

- Is there a possibility of this leading to paid employment?

SUPPORTED EMPLOYMENT

- Become familiar with supported employment services within the local area. Visit and talk to the providers – establish what model is being used. This will allow you to discuss employment support with confidence with the families and young people.

- Ensure that employment is discussed and encouraged as an outcome within the assessment process.

HOUSING OPTIONS

- Ensure that you seek the views separately of young people and their family about future living arrangements. Understanding early on the expectations of the young people and their families can help you to plan effectively and manage any potential conflicts.

- Consider ways you can feed information about potential accommodation needs to commissioners and budget holders, ensuring that there is sufficient time to plan for forthcoming accommodation needs and to accurately reflect potential future costings.

- Encourage young people and their carers to think early on about what their future accommodation plans may be.

- Consider where you can access appropriate information about housing options, and encourage young people to explore these with their family if they are thinking of leaving home in the future. Look at whether information on housing options is published as part of the Local Offer.

- Meet with commissioners and senior management and ask for support to coordinate supported living projects or query with your line manager how this could be done as part of the transition process. Find out how they convey the housing needs of young people coming through transition to prospective providers.

- Encourage all young people you work with to complete a one-page profile, and find out about support offered by local advocacy services for matching up people to share accommodation.

- Identify a link within local housing that could support with access to social housing.

Working effectively with young people in transition is complex and multifaceted, and actually pulls together many key themes, explored throughout the chapters here. Case studies have been used to clarify the points raised to provide a thorough understanding of the issues around personalisation, housing, health, SEN, children's services, employment, carers and mental capacity.

A career in transition can be challenging, complex and frustrating, but it can also be hugely rewarding and satisfying when the young person has been actively involved in their transition, rather than having it happen to them, and when they have experienced a positive transition and are living a life which they have choice and control over, enjoying the same opportunities that are available to other young people of their age.

APPENDIX 1: INFORMATION ON BENEFITS FOR PEOPLE WITH DISABILITIES

GENERAL BENEFITS

Benefit	Description	Eligibility
Employment and Support Allowance (ESA)	An allowance that offers you: • financial support if you are unable to work • personalised help so that you can work if you are able to. You get an assessment rate for 13 weeks after your claim. There are two different rates depending on if you are under or over 25. After 13 weeks, if you are entitled to ESA, you will be placed in one of two groups: a work-related activity group or a support group.	You may be eligible if your illness or disability affects your ability to work and you are: • under State Pension age • not getting Statutory Sick Pay or Statutory Maternity Pay and you have not gone back to work • not getting Jobseeker's Allowance. Usually your ESA is not affected if you are doing 'permitted work'. This allows you to: • work and earn up to a set amount each week • work and earn up to a set amount each week doing work as part of a treatment programme, or supervised by someone from a local council or voluntary organisation • work less than 16 hours a week, and earn up to a set amount each week for up to 52 weeks. You can also do 'supported permitted work' and earn up to a set amount each week if your illness or disability very severely limits your ability to work. There is no limit to the number of hours per week or length of time you can do supported permitted work. Supported permitted work is supervised by someone from a local council or a voluntary organisation whose job it is to arrange work for people with disabilities. Any volunteer work you do needs to be reported, but it does not normally affect your ESA.

		Your income may affect your income-related or contribution-based ESA. Income can include: • you and your partner's income • savings over a set amount. You will not be eligible for income-related ESA if you get Universal Credit.
Jobseeker's Allowance (JSA)	An allowance to help you while you look for work. How much you get depends on your circumstances. A work coach will help you make a work plan for how you are going to find a job. You must go to a Jobcentre Plus office (usually every two weeks or when asked). This is known as 'signing on'. When you sign on, you will need to show your work coach what you have been doing to look for work, e.g. job applications and interviews. There are two types of JSA: contribution-based and income-based. You will get contribution-based JSA if you have paid enough National Insurance contributions in the two tax years before the year you are claiming in. You will get income-based JSA if you have earned a low income or have not worked over the last two years.	To be eligible, all of the following must apply. You must: • be 18 or over but below State Pension age – there are some exceptions if you are 16 or 17 • not be in full-time education • living in England, Scotland or Wales • be available for work • be actively seeking work • work on average less than 16 hours per week. You must also go to a JSA interview after you apply.

cont.

Benefit	Description	Eligibility
Income Support	An amount of money to supplement income. You get a basic payment (personal allowance) and extra payments (premiums) depending on your circumstances.	To be eligible, all of the following must apply. You must: • be between 16 and Pension Credit-qualifying age • be pregnant, or a carer, or a lone parent with a child under five or, in some cases, unable to work because you are sick or have a disability • have no income or a low income (your partner's income and savings will be taken into account) • be working less than 16 hours a week (and your partner works less than 24 hours a week) • living in England, Scotland or Wales.
Working Tax Credit	An amount of money to supplement income. You get a basic amount and extra (known as 'elements') on top of this depending on your circumstances and income.	You may be eligible if you are: • aged between 16 and 24 and have a child or a qualifying disability • 25 or over, with or without children. You must: • work a set number of hours each week • get paid for the work you do (or expect to) • have an income below a set level.
Council Tax reduction	A discount on your Council Tax bill. What you get depends on: • where you live – each council runs its own scheme • your circumstances (e.g. income, number of children, benefits, residency status) • your household income – this includes savings, pensions and your partner's income • if your children live with you • if other adults live with you.	You may be eligible if you are on a low income or claim benefits. Your bill could be reduced by up to 100%. You can apply if you own your home, rent, are unemployed or working.

Housing Benefit	Helps pay for your rent if you are on a low income. Housing Benefit can pay for part or all of your rent. How much you get depends on your income and circumstances.	You may be eligible if: • you pay rent • you are on a low income or claiming benefits • your savings are below a set level. You can apply for Housing Benefit whether you are unemployed or working, but if you live with a partner, only one of you can get Housing Benefit. If you are single and under 35, you can only get Housing Benefit for bed-sit accommodation or a single room in shared accommodation.
Universal Credit	Universal Credit is being introduced in stages and is currently only available in a few areas. It is replacing: • JSA • Housing Benefit • Working Tax Credit • Child Tax Credit • ESA • Income Support. You do not need to do anything if you are already claiming any benefits. You will be told when Universal Credit will affect you.	You may be able to claim if you are eligible and you live in: • Bath • Hammersmith, London • Harrogate • Inverness • North West England • Shotton, Wales.

BENEFITS TO HELP WITH A DISABILITY

Benefit	Description	Eligibility
Blind Person's Allowance	An extra amount of tax-free allowance, so you can earn more before paying tax.	England and Wales: You are eligible if you are registered with the local council as blind or severely sight impaired. Scotland and Northern Ireland: You are eligible if you cannot do work that requires eyesight.

Disability premiums (Income Support)	An extra amount added to your Income Support. There are three levels of these premiums – basic, severe and enhanced – and two rates for single people and couples.	To be eligible you must be:
		• under Pension Credit age
		• either registered blind or getting:
		  ▫ Disability Living Allowance
		  ▫ Personal Independence Payment
		  ▫ Working Tax Credit with a disability element.

Disabled Facilities Grant	A council grant to help with changes to your home, e.g. • widen doors and install ramps • improve access to rooms and facilities, e.g. stair lift or a downstairs bathroom • provide a heating system suitable for your needs • adapt heating or lighting controls to make them easier to use.	To be eligible you must: • own the property or be a tenant • intend to live in the property during the grant period (currently five years). Landlords with tenants with disabilities can also apply.

Disabled Students' Allowance (DSA)	An allowance for students with disabilities in higher education. It is paid on top of other student finance and does not have to be repaid. You can get help with the costs of: - specialist equipment, like computer software - non-medical helpers, like a note-taker or reader - extra travel because of your disability - other things related to your studies, like photocopying.	You may be eligible if you have a: - disability or long-term health condition - mental health condition - specific learning difficulty like dyslexia or dyspraxia. You must also: - be an undergraduate or postgraduate student (including Open University or distance learning) - have a condition that affects your ability to study - qualify for student finance from Student Finance England - be studying a course that lasts at least a year.
Personal Independence Payment (PIP)	This helps with some of the extra costs caused by long-term ill health or a disability if you are aged 16–64. The rate depends on how your condition affects you, not the condition itself. You will need an assessment to work out the level of help you get. Your award will be regularly re-assessed to make sure you are getting the right support. PIP is tax-free and you can get it whether you are in or out of work. It is made up of two components – daily living and mobility – each with two rates: standard and enhanced. Whether you get one or both of these depends on how your condition affects you.	To be eligible you must: - be aged 16–64 - have a long-term health condition or disability and difficulties with activities related to 'daily living' and or mobility - be in Great Britain when you claim – there are some exceptions, e.g. members and family members of the Armed Forces - have been in Great Britain for at least two of the last three years - be habitually resident in the UK, Ireland, Isle of Man or the Channel Islands - not be subject to immigration control (unless you are a sponsored immigrant).

BENEFITS FOR CARERS

Benefit	Description	Eligibility
Carer's Allowance	Carer's Allowance is to help you look after someone with substantial caring needs. It is taxable and can affect other benefits including those of the person you care for. You cannot receive Carer's Allowance at the same time as another income-replacement benefit (e.g. a pension), but it could mean you are entitled to more with your other benefit.	You might be eligible if all of the following apply: • You are 16 or over. • You spend at least 35 hours per week caring for someone, but you do not have to be related to or live with them. • You have been in England, Scotland or Wales for at least two of the last three years. • You normally live in England, Scotland or Wales, or you live abroad as a member of the Armed Forces • You are not in full-time education or studying for more than 21 hours a week. • You earn less than a set amount each week. • The person you care for must be receiving one of: ▫ PIP ▫ DLA.
Carer's Credit	A National Insurance credit that helps to build your National Insurance contributions if you have to take on caring responsibilities. This means you have no gaps in your National Insurance record, and helps you build up your entitlement to a State Pension.	You might be eligible if all of the following apply: • You are 16 or over. • You are under State Pension age. • You are looking after someone for at least 20 hours per week. • The person you care for must be receiving one of: ▫ PIP ▫ DLA.

BENEFITS TO HELP WITH EMPLOYMENT IF YOU HAVE A DISABILITY

Benefit	Description	Eligibility
Access to Work	A grant to pay for practical support if you have a disability, health or mental health condition to help you start work, stay in work or move into self-employment or start a business. It is not for business start-up costs, and you cannot get a grant for voluntary work. The money does not have to be paid back, and will not affect other benefits. It can pay for: • adaptations to the equipment you use • special equipment • fares to work if you are unable to use public transport • a support worker or job coach to help you in your workplace • a support service if you have a mental health condition and you are absent from work or finding it difficult to work • disability awareness training for your colleagues • a communicator at a job interview • the cost of moving your equipment if you change location or job.	To be eligible you must be 16 or over and either: • about to start work or a work trial • be in a paid job or self-employed Your disability/health condition/mental health must affect your ability to do a job. You might not qualify if you receive: • ESA • Income Support • National Insurance credits.

cont.

Benefit	Description	Eligibility
Work Choice	Work Choice can help you get and keep a job if you have a disability and find it hard to work. It is voluntary – you do not have to do it. The type of support you get depends on the help you need. This is different for everyone, but can include: - training and developing your skills - building your confidence - finding a job that suits you - interview coaching.	To be eligible you must: - be of working age - need support in work as well as to find a job - be able to work at least 16 hours a week after work entry support - have a recognised disability that means you find it hard to get or keep a job - need specialist help that you cannot get from other government programmes or schemes, e.g. workplace adjustments, suppliers working in partnership with Jobcentre Plus or Access to Work. You can apply if you have a job but are at risk of losing it because of your disability. This also applies if you are self-employed. You do not have to be getting benefits to apply.

APPENDIX 2: ONE-PAGE PROFILE SAMPLE

PHOTO

What makes me happy:

- _____

- _____

- _____

- _____

- _____

- _____

What people like and admire about me:

- _____

- _____

- _____

- _____

- _____

- _____

How I want to be supported:

- _____

- _____

- _____

- _____

- _____

- _____

REFERENCES

Abraham, K. and Aldridge, J. (2010) *The Mental Well-being of Young Carers in Manchester*. Loughborough and Manchester: Young Carers Research Group with Manchester Carers Forum and Child and Adolescent Mental Health Services.

Ahmed, M. (2009) 'CSCI: Personalisation not a reality for many with complex needs.' *Community Care*, 26 January. Available at www.communitycare.co.uk/2009/01/26/csci-personalisation-not-a-reality-for-many-with-complex-needs, accessed on 7 January 2015.

Alakeson, V. (2014) *Delivering Personal Health Budgets: A Guide to Policy and Practice*. Bristol: Policy Press.

Asmussen, K. (2011) *The Evidence-based Parenting Practitioner's Handbook*. Abingdon: Routledge.

Atherton, A. and Crickmore, D. (2011) *Learning Disabilities: Towards Inclusion*. Edinburgh: Elsevier.

Atkinson, D., Jackson, M. and Walmsley, J. (1997) *Forgotten Lives: Exploring the History of Learning Disability*. Kidderminster: BILD.

Audit Commission (2007) *Out of Authority Placements for Special Educational Needs*. London: Audit Commission for local authorities and the National Health Service in England. Available at http://archive.audit-commission.gov.uk/auditcommission/subwebs/publications/studies/studyPDF/3369.pdf, accessed on 7 January 2015.

Baker, C. (2011) *Permanence and Stability for Disabled Looked After Children*. Iriss Insights, No. 11, May. Available at www.iriss.org.uk/resources/permanence-and-stability-disabled-looked-after-children, accessed on 7 January 2015.

Baker, G.A. and Jacoby, A. (eds) (2000) *Quality of Life in Epilepsy: Beyond Seizure Counts in Assessment and Treatment*. Amsterdam: Harwood Academic Publishers.

Beadle-Brown, J., Guest, C., Richardson, L., Malovic, A., Bradshaw, J. and Himmerich, J. (2013) *Living in Fear: Better Outcomes for People with Learning Disabilities and Autism. Executive Summary*. Canterbury: Tizard Centre, University of Kent. Available at www.mcch.org.uk/pages/multimedia/db_document.document?id=7848, accessed on 6 December 2014.

Beckett, C. (2006) *Essential Theory for Social Work Practice*. London: Sage.

Beresford, B. and Cavet, J. (2009) *Transitions to Adult Services by Disabled Young People Leaving Out of Authority Residential School*. York: Social Policy Research Unit, University of York. Available at http://php.york.ac.uk/inst/spru/pubs/1195/, accessed on 7 January 2015.

Beresford, B., Moran, N., Sloper, T., Cusworth, L. *et al.* (2013) *Transition to Adult Services and Adulthood for Young People with Autistic Spectrum Conditions*. York: Social Policy Research Unit, University of York. Available at http://php.york.ac.uk/inst/spru/pubs/2371/, accessed on 7 January 2015.

BOND (Better Outcomes New Delivery) (2014) 'Children & young people with learning disabilities.' London: YoungMinds. Available at www.youngminds.org.uk/training_services/bond_voluntary_sector/resources/commissioners/1775_children_young_people_with_learning_disabilities, accessed on 7 January 2015.

Boylan, J. and Dalrymple, J. (2009) *Understanding Advocacy for Children and Young People*. Maidenhead: Open University Press.

Brammer, A. (2007) *Social Work Law*. 2nd edition. London: Pearson Education Ltd.

Brindle, D. (2013) 'Funding for residential training for disabled people in jeopardy.' *The Guardian*, 26 December. Available at www.theguardian.com/society/2013/dec/26/funding-residential-training-disabled-people-jeopardy, accessed on 8 October 2014.

Broadhurst, S., Yates, K. and Mullen, B. (2012) 'An evaluation of the My Way transition programme.' *Tizard Learning Disability Review 17*, 3, 124–134.

Brown, K. (2010) *Vulnerable Adults and Community Care.* 2nd edition. Exeter: Learning Matters.

Brown, R., Barber, P. and Martin, D. (2008) *The Mental Capacity Act 2005: A Guide for Practice.* Exeter: Learning Matters.

Carers Trust (2012) 'Key Facts About Carers.' London: Carers Trust. Available at www.carers.org/key-facts-about-carers, accessed on 5 October 2014.

Carers Trust (n.d.) 'Carer's Assessment.' London: Carers Trust. Available at www.carers.org/carers-assessment, accessed on 12 January 2015.

Carers UK (2014) *Your Right to Flexible Working.* London: Carers UK. Available at www.carersuk.org/help-and-advice/work-and-career/your-right-to-flexible-working, accessed on 8 October 2014.

Carers UK (n.d.) 'Carer's Allowance.' Available at www.carersuk.org/search/carers-allowance, accessed on 15 January 2015.

Carnaby, S. (2002) *Learning Disability Today: Key Issues for Providers, Managers, Practitioners and Users.* Brighton: Pavilion.

Carpenter, B. (1997) 'Finding the Family: Early Intervention and the Families of Children with Special Educational Needs.' In B. Carpenter (ed.) *Emerging Trends in Family Support and Early Intervention.* London: David Fulton Publishers.

Children's Society (2013) *Hidden from View: The Experiences of Young Carers in England.* Available at www.childrenssociety.org.uk/sites/default/files/tcs/report_hidden-from-view_young-carers_final.pdf, accessed on 10 March 2015.

Cocker, C. and Allain, L. (2008) *Social Work with Looked After Children.* Transforming Social Work Practice Series. Exeter: Learning Matters.

Cohen, D. (2013) *The Care Bill: A Summary.* Health & Social Care Partnership. London: Sitra. Available at www.sitra.org/documents/care-bill-2013/, accessed on 7 January 2015.

Committee of Enquiry into the Education of Handicapped Children and Young People (1978) *Special Educational Needs: The Warnock Report.* London: HMSO Available at www.educationengland.org.uk/documents/warnock/warnock1978.html, accessed on 7 January 2015.

CQC (Care Quality Commission) (2014) *From the Pond into the Sea. Children's Transition to Adult Health Services.* London: CQC. Available at www.cqc.org.uk/sites/default/files/CQC_Transition%20Report_Summary_lores.pdf, accessed on 7 January 2015.

Dare, A. and O'Donovan, M. (2002) *Good Practice in Caring for Young Children with Special Needs.* 2nd edition. Cheltenham: Nelson Thornes.

Davey, V., Fernandez, J., Knapp, M., Vick, N., *et al.* (2007) *Direct Payments: A National Survey of Direct Payments Policy and Practice.* London: Personal Social Services Research Unit.

DCA (Department for Constitutional Affairs) (2007) *Mental Capacity Act 2005 Code of Practice.* London: The Stationary Office. Available at www.gov.uk/government/uploads/system/uploads/attachment_data/file/224660/Mental_Capactiy_Act_code_of_practice.pdf, accessed on 6 May 2015.

DCLG (Department for Communities and Local Government) (2012) *Allocation of Accommodation: Guidance for Local Housing Authorities in England.* London: DCLG. Available at www.gov.uk/government/publications/allocation-of-accommodation-guidance-for-local-housing-authorities-in-england, accessed on 7 January 2015.

DCSF (Department for Children, Schools and Families) and DH (Department of Health) (2007) *A Transition Guide for All Services: Key Information for Professionals about the Transition Process for Disabled Young People.* Nottingham: DCSF Publications. Available at www.transitioninfonetwork.org.uk/media/2490/transition_guide_for_all_services.pdf, accessed on 7 January 2015.

Dean, J. (2003) *Unaddressed: The Housing Aspirations of Young Disabled People in Scotland.* Glasgow and York: University of Glasgow for the Joseph Rowntree Foundation. Available at www.jrf.org.uk/sites/files/jrf/1859351468.pdf, accessed on 7 January 2015.

Dee, L. (2006) *Improving Transition Planning for Young People with Special Educational Needs.* Maidenhead: Open University Press.

DfE (Department for Education) (1994) *Code of Practice on the Identification and Assessment of Special Education Needs.* London: DFE and Welsh Office.

DfE (2010) *Evaluation of the Staying Put: 18 Plus Family Placement Programme: Final Report.* Available at www.gov.uk/government/uploads/system/uploads/attachment_data/file/183518/DFE-RR191.pdf, accessed on 6 December 2014.

DfE (2011) *Support and Aspiration: A New Approach to Special Educational Needs and Disability.* London: The Stationery Office. Available at http://webarchive.nationalarchives.gov.uk/20130401151715/https://www.education.gov.uk/publications/standard/publicationdetail/page1/cm%208027, accessed on 8 January 2015.

DfE (2010) *The Children Act 1989 Guidance and Regulations. Volume 3: Planning Transition to Adulthood for Care Leavers.* Available at www.gov.uk/government/uploads/system/uploads/attachment_data/file/397649/CA1989_Transitions_guidance.pdf, accessed on 17 March 2015.

DfE (2014) The Young Person's Guide to the Children and Families Act 2014. London: HMSO.

DfES (Department for Education and Skills) (2001) *SEN Toolkit: Section 10: Transition Planning.* Nottingham: DfES Publications. Available at http://webarchive.nationalarchives.gov.uk/20130401151715/http://www.education.gov.uk/publications/eOrderingDownload/DfES-0558-2001-2.pdf, accessed on 7 January 2015.

DfES (2004) *Every Child Matters: Change for Children.* London: The Stationery Office.

DfES (2004) *Removing Barriers to Achievement: The Government's Strategy for SEN.* London: The Stationery Office. Available at http://webarchive.nationalarchives.gov.uk/20130401151715/http://www.education.gov.uk/publications/standard/publicationDetail/Page1/DfES%200117%202004, accessed on 7 January 2015.

DH (Department of Health) (1999) *Caring about Carers: A National Strategy for Carers.* London: DH. Available at http://webarchive.nationalarchives.gov.uk/20130107105354/http://www.dh.gov.uk/en/Publicationsandstatistics/Publications/PublicationsPolicyAndGuidance/DH_4006522, accessed on 7 January 2015.

DH (2001) *Valuing People – A New Strategy for Learning Disability for the 21st Century.* London: The Stationery Office. Available at www.gov.uk/government/uploads/system/uploads/attachment_data/file/250877/5086.pdf, accessed on 8 January 2015.

DH (2003) *Fair Access to Care Services – Guidance on Eligibility Criteria for Adult Social Care.* London: DH.

DH (2004) *National Service Framework for Children, Young People and Maternity Services.* London: The Stationery Office. Available at www.gov.uk/government/uploads/system/uploads/attachment_data/file/199952/National_Service_Framework_for_Children_Young_People_and_Maternity_Services_-_Core_Standards.pdf, accessed on 8 January 2015.

DH (2005) *Independence, Well-being and Choice: Our Vision for the Future of Social Care for Adults in England.* Social Care Green Paper. London: DH. Available at http://webarchive.nationalarchives.gov.uk/+/www.dh.gov.uk/en/Consultations/Closedconsultations/DH_4116631, accessed on 9 January 2015.

DH (2006) *Our Health, Our Care, Our Say: A New Direction for Community Services.* London: DH. Available at http://webarchive.nationalarchives.gov.uk/+/dh.gov.uk/en/publicationsandstatistics/publications/publicationspolicyandguidance/dh_4127453, accessed on 9 January 2015.

DH (2007a) *Good Practice in Learning Disability Nursing.* London: The Stationery Office.

DH (2007b) *The Mental Capacity Act Deprivation of Liberty Safeguards.* London: The Stationery Office.

DH (2008) *Refocusing the Care Programme Approach: Policy and Positive Practice Guidance.* London: The Stationery Office.

DH (2009a) *Valuing People Now: A New Three-year Strategy for People with Learning Disabilities.* London: The Stationery Office. Available at http://webarchive.nationalarchives.gov.uk/20130107105354/http://www.dh.gov.uk/en/Publicationsandstatistics/Publications/PublicationsPolicyAndGuidance/DH_093377, accessed on 9 January 2015.

DH (2009b) *Valuing People Now: Summary Report March 2009 to September 2010.* London: The Stationery Office.

DH (2010) *Person-centred Planning: Advice for Using Person-centred Thinking, Planning and Reviews in Schools and Transition.* London: The Stationery Office.

DH (2011) *Pathways to Getting a Life: Transition Planning for Full Lives.* London: The Stationery Office.

DH (2012) *National Framework for NHS Continuing Healthcare and NHS-funded Nursing Care.* London: The Stationary Office.

DH (2013a) *The Care Bill – Transition for Children to Adult Care and Support Services.* Factsheet 11. London: DH.

DH (2013b) *Adult Social Care Outcomes Framework 2014 to 2015.* London: DH.

DH, DfEE and Home Office (2000) *Framework for the Assessment of Children in Need and their Families.* London: The Stationery Office. Available at http://webarchive.nationalarchives.gov.uk/20130401151715/https:/www.education.gov.uk/publications/eOrderingDownload/Framework%20for%20the%20assessment%20of%20children%20in%20need%20and%20their%20families.pdf, accessed on 8 January 2015.

DH Partnerships for Children, Families and Maternity (2008) *Transition: Moving on Well.* London: DH. Available at http://webarchive.nationalarchives.gov.uk/20130107105354/http://www.dh.gov.uk/prod_consum_dh/groups/dh_digitalassets/@dh/@en/documents/digitalasset/dh_083593.pdf, accessed on 8 January 2015.

DHSS (Department of Health and Social Security) (1971) *Better Services for the Mentally Handicapped.* London: The Stationery Office.

DWP (2013a) *Preparing for Adulthood Factsheet: Supported Internships.* Bath: Preparing for Adulthood Programme. Available at www.preparingforadulthood.org.uk/resources/pfa-resources/factsheet-supported-internships, accessed on 7 January 2015.

DWP (2013b) *Preparing for Adulthood Factsheet: Access to Work.* Bath: Preparing for Adulthood Programme.

DWP (2014) 'Disability Confident campaign.' Available at www.gov.uk/government/collections/disability-confident-campaign, accessed on 9 January 2015.

Emerson, E. and Einfield, S. L. (2001) *Challenging Behaviour.* Cambridge: Cambridge University Press.

Emerson, E. and Hatton, C. (2008) *Estimating Future Need for Adult Social Care Services for People with a Learning Disability in England.* Lancaster: Centre for Disability Research, University of Lancaster.

Evans, C. and Tippins, E. (2008) *Foundations of Nursing: An Integrated Approach.* Maidenhead: McGraw-Hill Education.

Fiedler, B. (2006) *Improving Outcomes for Service Users in Adult Placement: Commissioning and Care Management.* SCIE Guide 14. Available at www.scie.org.uk/publications/guides/guide14/files/guide14.pdf, accessed on 6 December 2014.

Foundation for People with Learning Disabilities (2011) *Learning Disability Statistics: Children.* Available at www.learningdisabilities.org.uk, accessed on 10 October 2014.

Foxwell, T. (2010) *COPE: The Directory of Post-16 Residential Education and Training for Young People with Special Needs.* 13th edition. Wiltshire: Lifetime Publishing.

Franklin, S. and Sanderson, H. (2014) *Personalisation in Practice: Supporting Young People with Disabilities through the Transition to Adulthood.* London: Jessica Kingsley Publishers.

Gabbitas Education (2005) *Schools for Special Needs: A Complete Guide.* London: Kogan Page.

Gabbitas Education (2013) *Schools for Special Needs 2014: The Complete Guide to Special Needs Education in the United Kingdom.* London: Kogan Page.

GAL (Getting a Life), HAS (Helen Sanderson Associates) and NDTi (National Development Team for inclusion) (2011) *Pathways to Getting a Life: Transition Planning for Full Lives*. Bath and Stockport: GAL, HAS and NDTi. Available at www.ndti.org.uk/uploads/files/2011-Pathways-to-getting-a-life.pdf, accessed on 7 January 2015.

Gates, B. and Barr, O. (2009) *Oxford Handbook of Learning and Intellectual Disability Nursing*. Oxford: Oxford University Press.

Gates, B. and Atherton, H. (2007) *Learning Disabilities: Toward Inclusion*. 5th edition. London: Churchill Livingstone Elsevier.

Giraud-Saunders, A. (2012) *What Do I Need to Know about NHS Continuing Healthcare? Information for Families of People with Learning Disabilities*. London: Foundation for People with Learning Disabilities. Available at www.netbuddy.org.uk/static/cms_page_media/164/NHS_CHC-2.pdf, accessed on 7 January 2015.

Glendinning, C. *et al.* (2008) 'Increasing choice and control for older and disabled people: A critical review of new developments in England.' *Social Policy and Administration* 42, 5, 451–469.

Gross, J. (2013) *Beating Bureaucracy in Special Educational Needs*. 2nd edition. Abingdon: Routledge.

Haaken, J. and Reavey, P. (eds) (2010) *Memory Matters: Contexts for Understanding Sexual Abuse Recollections*. Hove: Routledge.

Halliwell, M. (2003) *Supporting Children with Special Educational Needs: A Guide for Assistants in Schools and Pre-Schools*. Abingdon: David Fulton Publishers.

Hardie, E. and Tilly, L. (2012) *An Introduction to Supporting People with a Learning Disability*. London: Learning Matters.

Hardy, R. (2014) 'Shared lives: Community-based approach to supporting adults.' *The Guardian*, 23 May. Available at www.theguardian.com/social-care-network/2014/may/23/shared-lives-community-based-supporting-adults, accessed on 6 December 2014.

HM Government (2003) *Every Child Matters*. London: The Stationery Office. Available at www.education.gov.uk/consultations/downloadableDocs/EveryChildMatters.pdf, accessed on 8 January 2015.

Heslop, P., Abbott, D., Johnson, L. and Mallet, R. (2007) *Help to Move On: Transition Pathways for Young People with Learning Difficulties in Residentials Schools and Colleges*. Bristol: Norah Fry Research Centre.

HM Government (2007) *Putting People First: A Shared Vision and Commitment to the Transformation of Adult Social Care*. London: The Stationery Office. Available at http://webarchive.nationalarchives.gov.uk/20130107105354/http://www.dh.gov.uk/prod_consum_dh/groups/dh_digitalassets/@dh/@en/documents/digitalasset/dh_081119.pdf, accessed on 7 January 2015.

Human Rights Joint Committee (2012) *Implementation of the Right of Disabled People to Independent Living. Twenty-third Report*. Available at www.publications.parliament.uk/pa/jt201012/jtselect/jtrights/257/25705.htm, accessed on 6 December 2014.

In Control (2012) *Seven Steps to Being in Control*. Available at www.in-control.org.uk/support/support-for-individuals-family-members-carers/seven-steps-to-being-in-control.aspx, accessed on 7 January 2015.

Jackson, L. (2010) 'Keeping adult social care in the family.' *The Guardian*, 3 November. Available at www.theguardian.com/society/2010/dec/03/keeping-adult-social-care-family, accessed on 6 December 2014.

Jarratt, S. (2012) *Developing the Transition Pathway for Young People with Learning Disabilities: Data Collection and Analysis Report*. Joint Improvement Partnership. Available at www.housingandsupport.org

Joint Committee on Human Rights (2008a) *A Life Like Any Other? Human Rights of Adults with Learning Disabilities*. London: The Stationery Office.

Joint Committee on Human Rights (2008b) Written Evidence. Memorandum from the National Autistic Society. Available at www.publications.parliament.uk/pa/jt200708/jtselect/jrights/40/40we103.htm, accessed 17 March 2015.

Jones, R. (2011) 'Successful fostering needs good social work support.' *The Guardian*, 18 May. Available at www.theguardian.com/society/joepublic/2011/may/18/fostering-needs-good-social-work-support, accessed on 6 December 2014.

Kaehne, A. and Beyer, S. (2011) 'Can transition meetings in school be done in a person-centred way?' *Learning Disability Today*, October/November. Available at www.careknowledge.com/uploadedfiles/redbox/ck/careknowledge_cms/public/journals/learning_disability_today/ldt-octnov11%20pg28-30.pdf, accessed on 7 January 2015.

Kennedy, J. (2014) *Independent Mental Capacity Advocacy Service.* Available at www.careknowledge.com/independent_mental_capacity_advocacy_service_25769807610.aspx, accessed on 10 March 2015.

Koprawska, J. (2010) *Communication and Interpersonal Skills in Social Work.* London: Learning Matters.

Lauerman, M. (2014) *Transitions, Part 1: The Planned and the Unplanned.* CareKnowledge Special Report No. 78. Hove: Pavilion Publishing and Media Ltd. Available at www.careknowledge.com/transitions_part_1_the_planned_and_the_unplanned_25769807518.aspx, accessed on 7 January 2015.

Leadbeater, C., Bartlett, J. and Gallagher, N. (2008) *Making it Personal.* London: Demos. Available at www.demos.co.uk/publications/makingitpersonal, accessed on 7 January 2015.

Learner, S. (2013) 'Tenants with learning difficulties face prejudice and lack of suitable housing.' *The Guardian*, 18 March. Available at www.theguardian.com/housing-network/2013/mar/18/learning-disability-prejudice-housing, accessed on 10 October 2014.

Lee, J. (2012) 'The SEN cliff edge.' *TES Magazine*, 12 October. Available at www.tes.co.uk/article.aspx?storycode=6295174, accessed on 7 January 2015.

Lissouer, T. and Clayden, G. (2011) *Illustrated Textbook of Paediatrics.* 4th edition. Philadelphia, PA: Mosby Ltd Elsevier.

Maxwell, Y. and King, N. (2006) *Enhancing Housing Choices for People with a Learning Disability.* Housing Learning & Improvement Network. Available at www.housinglin.org.uk/_library/Resources/Housing/Housing_advice/Enhancing_Housing_Choices_for_People_with_a_Learning_Disability.pdf, accessed on 6 December 2014.

Mednick, M. (2002) *Supporting Children with Multiple Disabilities.* Birmingham: Questions Publishing.

Mencap (2012) *Housing for People with a Learning Disability.* Available at www.mencap.org.uk/sites/default/files/documents/2012.108%20Housing%20report_V7.pdf, accessed on 6 December 2014.

Mencap (2014) *Employment.* Available at www.mencap.org.uk/all-about-learning-disability/information-professionals/employment, accessed on 9 September 2014.

Mencap (n.d.) 'Employ Me.' Available at www.mencap.org.uk/what-we-do/our-services/work/employ-me, accessed on 9 January 2015.

Merriman, S. (2009) *TransMap: From Theory into Practice: The Underlying Principles in Supporting Disabled Young People in Transition to Adulthood.* London: Council for Disabled Children.

Ministry of Justice (2008) *Mental Capacity Act 2005: Deprivation of Liberty Safeguards – Code of Practice to Supplement the Main Mental Capacity Act 2005 Code of Practice.* London: The Stationery Office. Available at http://webarchive.nationalarchives.gov.uk/20130107105354/http:/www.dh.gov.uk/en/Publicationsandstatistics/Publications/PublicationsPolicyAndGuidance/DH_085476, accessed on 12 January 2015.

Morris, J. (1999) *Hurtling into a Void: Transition to Adulthood for Young Disabled People with Complex Health and Support Needs.* Brighton: Joseph Rowntree Foundation.

Morris, J. (2002) *Moving into Adulthood: Young Disabled People Moving into Adulthood.* York: Joseph Rowntree Foundation. Available at www.jrf.org.uk/publications/moving-adulthood-young-disabled-people-moving-adulthood, accessed on 12 October 2014.

Murray, J. (2012) 'Residential college places for young disabled at risk.' *The Guardian*, 17 September. Available at www.theguardian.com/education/2012/sep/17/funding-for-disabled-specialist-colleges, accessed on 8 October 2014.

NAO (National Audit Office) (2011) *Oversight of Special Education for Young People Aged 16–25*. Available at www.nao.org.uk/report/oversight-of-special-education-for-young-people-aged-16-25/, accessed on 7 January 2015.

NCAS (National Care Advisory Service) (2009) *Journeys to Home: Care Leavers' Successful Transition to Independent Accommodation.* London: NCAS. Available at http://resources.leavingcare.org/uploads/3433e51041436ce0a61e0d68657e3513.pdf?utm_source=Keynotes+mailing+list&utm_campaign=51b4aaafcc-october_201010_1_2010&utm_medium=email, accessed on 7 January 2015.

NCB (National Children's Bureau) (2010) *Aiming High for Disabled Children.* VSS – Policy Briefing. Available at www.ncb.org.uk/media/42201/aiming_high_vssbriefing.pdf, accessed on 7 January 2015.

NDTi (National Development Team for inclusion) (2010) *The Real Tenancy Test – Tenancy Rights in Supported Living.* Bath: NDTi. Available at www.ndti.org.uk/uploads/files/The_Real_Tenancy_Test,_NDTi_September_20101.pdf, accessed on 6 December 2014.

NDTi (2011) *Insights 11 – Commissioning Employment Supports.* Available at www.ndti.org.uk/publications/ndti-insights/insights-11-commissioning-employment-supports, accessed on 7 January 2015.

NDTi (2013) *Insights 20 – Employment Support for Disabled People.* Available at www.ndti.org.uk/publications/ndti-insights/insights-20-employment-support-for-disabled-people2/, accessed on 7 January 2015.

New Horizons Partnership (2007) *What's a Social Enterprise?* Available at www.tandtwo.co.uk/social-enterprise.html, accessed on 17 March 2015.

NHS UK (2014) *Being a Young Carer.* Available at www.nhs.uk/CarersDirect/young/young/Pages/Overview.aspx, accessed on 5 October 2014.

ODI (Office for Disability Issues) and DWP (Department for Work and Pensions) (2013) *Fulfilling Potential: Making it Happen for Disabled People.* London: The Stationery Office.

ONS (Office for National Statistics) (2013) *Full Story: The Gender Gap in Unpaid Care Provision: is there an Impact on Health and Economic Position?* Available at www.ons.gov.uk/ons/dcp171776_310295.pdf, accessed on 10 March 2015.

Parker, C. (2014) *Transition to Adulthood: A Guide for Parents.* Carmarthen: Cerebra. Available at www.cerebra.org.uk/English/getinformation/guides%20for%20parents/Documents/Transition%20guide%20final%20web.pdf, accessed on 7 January 2015.

Parker, C., Honigmann, J. and Clements, L. (2013) *Transition to Adulthood: A Guide for Practitioners Working with Disabled Young People and their Families.* Carmarthen: Cebra. Available at http://base-uk.org/sites/base-uk.org/files/knowledge/Transition%20to%20Adulthood%20-%20guide%20for%20practitioners/cerebra_transitions_guide_for_professionals.pdf, accessed on 7 January 2015.

Patrick, R. (2014) 'Homing in on lack of housing choice.' *Disability Now.* Available at www.disabilitynow.org.uk/article/homing-lack-housing-choice, accessed on 6 December 2014.

Power, E. (2010) *Guerrilla Mum: Surviving the Special Educational Needs Jungle.* London: Jessica Kingsley Publishers.

Preparing for Adulthood programme (2015) *Supporting young people with mental health needs into employment: Practical guidance for commissioners.* Bath: Preparing for Adulthood. Available at www.ndti.org.uk/uploads/files/supporting_young_people_with_mental_health_problems_into_employment_practical_guidance_for_commissioners_final.pdf, accessed on 13 May 2015.

RCN (Royal College of Nursing) (2013) *Adolescent Transition Care. RCN Guidance for Nursing Staff.* London: RCN. Available at www.rcn.org.uk/__data/assets/pdf_file/0011/78617/004510.pdf, accessed on 7 January 2015.

Read, J., Clements, L.J. and Ruebain, D. (2006) *Disabled Children and the Law: Research and Good Practice.* 2nd edition. London: Jessica Kingsley Publishers.

RIPFA (Research in Practice for Adults) (2013) *Good Decision-making: Practitioners' Handbook.* Totnes: RIPFA.

Robinson, C. (2000) 'Transition and Change in the Lives of Families with a Young Disabled Child: The Early Years.' In D. May (ed.) *Transition and Change in the Lives of People with Intellectual Disabilities*. London: Jessica Kingsley Publishers.

Samuel, M. (2010) 'The future of employment support for people with disabilities.' *Community Care*, 20 August. Available at www.communitycare.co.uk/2010/08/20/the-future-of-employment-support-for-people-with-disabilities, accessed on 10 October 2014.

Samuel, M. (2012) 'Families' rights and responsibilities under the Mental Capacity Act.' *Community Care*, 24 July. Available at www.communitycare.co.uk/blogs/adult-care-blog/2012/07/families-rights-and-responsibilities-under-mental-capacity-act/, accessed on 7 January 2015.

Sanderson, H., Sholl, C. and Jordan, L. (n.d.) *Person-centred Transition*. Available at www.helensandersonassociates.co.uk/media/11296/person_centred_transition.pdf, accessed on 12 October 2014.

SCIE (Social Care Institute for Excellence) (2004) *The Road Ahead – Literature Review*. London and Bristol: Social Care Institute for Excellence and Norah Fry Research Centre. Available at www.scie.org.uk/publications/tra/literature/index.asp, accessed on 9 October 2014.

SCIE (2013) *Fair Access to Care Services (FACS): Prioritising Eligibility for Care and Support*. SCIE Guide 33. London: SCIE. Available at www.scie.org.uk/publications/guides/guide33/, accessed on 12 October 2014.

Silas, D. (2014) *A Guide to the SEN Code of Practice: What You Need to Know*. Available at www.aguidetothesencodeofpractice.co.uk/, accessed on 12 October 2014.

Social Enterprise UK (2014) *What are Social Enterprises?* Available at www.socialenterprise.org.uk/about/about-social-enterprise, accessed on 1 October 2014.

Southall, A. (2005) *Consultation in Child and Adolescent Mental Health Services*. Abingdon: Radcliffe Publishing.

Tassoni, P., Beith, K., Bulman, K. and Eldridge, H. (2007) *Child Care and Education: CACHE Level 3*. 4th edition. Oxford: Heinemann.

Tod, J., Castle, F. and Blamires, M. (1998) *Individual Education Plans Implementing Effective Practice*. Abingdon: Routledge.

Tomlinson, P. and Philpot, T. (2008) *A Child's Journey to Recovery: Assessment and Planning with Traumatized Children*. London: Jessica Kingsley Publishers.

Townsley, R. and Marriott, A. (2010) 'More than giving people a voice…' *Learning Disability Today 10*, 5, June, 35–37.

Waddell, G., Burton, A. K. *et al.* (2006) *Health and Work – Workplace, Healthcare Worker*. London: The Stationery Office.

Warner, H. K. (2006) *Meeting the Needs of Children with Disabilities: Families and Professionals Facing the Challenge together*. Abingdon: Routledge.

Williams, P. (2006) *Social Work with People with Learning Difficulties*. Transforming Social Work Practice Series. Exeter: Learning Matters.

Wilson, K. and James, A. (2007) *The Child Protection Handbook: The Practitioner's Guide to Safeguarding Children*. 3rd edition. Philadelphia, PA: Ballière Tindall Elsevier.

LIST OF ACTS AND CASES

Adoption and Children Act 2002. London: The Stationery Office.

Care Act 2014. London: The Stationery Office.

Carers (Equal Opportunities) Act 2004. London: The Stationery Office.

Carers (Recognition and Services) Act 1995. London: HMSO.

Carers and Disabled Children Act 2000. London: The Stationery Office.

Children Act 1989. London: HMSO.

Children Act 2004. London: The Stationery Office.

Children and Families Act 2014. London: The Stationery Office.

Children Leaving Care Act 2000. London: HMSO

Direct Payment Act 1996. London: HMSO

Disability Discrimination Act 1995. London: HMSO.

Disability Discrimination Act 2005. London: The Stationery Office.

Disability Discrimination Act 2010. London: The Stationery Office.

Draft Care and Support Bill 2012. London: The Stationery Office.

Education Act 1994. London: HMSO

Education Act 1981. London: HMSO.

Education Act 1996. London: The Stationery Office.

Education and Skills Act 2008. London: HMSO

Education and Inspections Act 2006. London: HMSO

Special Educational Needs and Disability Act 2001. London: The Stationery Office.

Equality Act 2010. London: The Stationery Office.

Learning and Skills Act 2000. London: The Stationery Office.

Localism Act 2001. London: The Stationery Office.

Mental Capacity Act 2005. London: The Stationery Office.

Mental Health Act 1983. London: HMSO.

National Health Service (NHS) and Community Care Act 1990. London: HMSO.

Welfare Reform Act 2012. London: The Stationery Office.

Cheshire West & Chester Council v P [2011] EWCA Civ 1257.

SUBJECT INDEX

AUTHOR INDEX